The Two Ma[jorities]

And Some Other Asp[ects]

Hilaire Belloc

Alpha Editions

This edition published in 2024

ISBN : 9789362519221

Design and Setting By
Alpha Editions
www.alphaedis.com
Email - info@alphaedis.com

As per information held with us this book is in Public Domain.
This book is a reproduction of an important historical work. Alpha Editions uses the best technology to reproduce historical work in the same manner it was first published to preserve its original nature. Any marks or number seen are left intentionally to preserve its true form.

Contents

FOREWORD .... - 1 -
THE TWO MAPS OF EUROPE .... - 2 -
NUMBERS IN WAR .... - 16 -
SUPPLY .... - 29 -
WAR TO-DAY AND YESTERDAY .... - 39 -
WHAT TO BELIEVE IN WAR NEWS .... - 51 -
WHAT THE WAR HAS TAUGHT US .... - 59 -

FOREWORD

THE six chapters of this little book discuss and explain six separate and most important phases of the present war. Every effort has been made to deal with the headings selected as comprehensively and as simply as possible, and it is hoped that, in this convenient form, the handbook will be welcomed by those who wish to follow the campaign with understanding. The various articles reprinted were written during the winter of the present year (1914-15), and many of the conclusions reached apply, therefore, to that period of the war only.

THE TWO MAPS OF EUROPE

Wherein the map of Europe, as it will be if Germany wins, is clearly defined and compared with the map of Europe re-arranged in accordance with the ideals of the Allies.

THE TWO MAPS OF EUROPE

IT is everywhere admitted that the result of the great war must be either, upon the whole, to produce a new map of Europe upon the German model, or a new map of Europe upon the model suitable to the ideas of the Allies.

By this it is not meant that either ideal will be completely reached, but that in the settlement one or the other will certainly preponderate. Indeed, it is in the struggle between these two new maps of Europe as ideals that the motive of the war consists.

Now, before attempting to determine in a graphic fashion what those two ideals are—before, that is, trying to draw two maps which shall represent respectively the German goal and the goal of the Allies, we must lay down certain postulates which are not always recognized but which are certainly true.

Unless we recognize their truth we shall come to accept wild statements, and to be frightened of those ridiculous prophecies which propose the extermination of Germany on the one hand, or the rule of the German government over England or France on the other.

I. The first of these postulates is that a modern European nation no longer desires to *annex* white men in Europe, and the territory they inhabit.

The example of Alsace-Lorraine alone has proved a sufficient lesson; the continued vitality of Poland after a hundred years has proved another, and even the difficulties of the Austro-Hungarian governments, with their subject races, a third. This does not mean that a modern European government would not annex in any circumstance. The possession of some all-important military or commercial point might occasionally make the perilous experiment worth while. But it means that the idea of annexation as an obvious corollary to military success has disappeared.

II. The second postulate is as follows: It is universally recognized—by the Germans quite as much as by ourselves—that the political boundaries so long established in Europe hardly ever correspond to exact national groupings, and very often violently conflict with the realities of national life.

No one is so foolish, for instance, as to pretend that the Finnish provinces of Russia are not quite separate from the rest of the Czar's dominions in tradition, and consciousness, and habit, and all the rest that makes a nation. No one in England now denies the existence of an Irish nationality.

No one, to take an Eastern case, would pretend that the Serbian feeling of nationality was not very real, and was very far from being contained by the present boundaries of Serbia.

The excuse for the old point of view—the point of view that political boundaries were sufficient and that the true nationalities which they cut through or suppressed might be neglected—was that in time, with the modern rapidity of communication and the power of the modern State, these divergent elements would be *absorbed*, or *digested into*, the greater nationality which governed them. But experience has falsified this very reasonable conception. It has been found not only that this transformation did not take place, but even that the old real nationalities were actually getting stronger. Poland, for instance, artificially cut through by the German, Austrian, and Russian frontiers, did seem for a time as though it were going to spring into a Russian, a German, and an Austrian type of Polish men; and in the latter case, that of Austria, some considerable advance was made towards such a result. But generations passed, and the process did not continue; on the contrary, the tide began to set backwards, and the conception of a united Poland is far stronger to-day even in the small and successful Austrian portion of Poland than it was thirty years ago.

In the face of these two postulates, the true national groupings have discovered their power and have already begun to appear in real form, as it were, through the artificial political boundaries which divided or suppressed them. Any one, the Germans as much as the rest, proposing to reconstruct Europe must most certainly take account of such realities, and must deal with the many national groups of Europe as the stones out of which the new building is to be erected.

But the particular way in which those stones may be used, the combinations into which they may be grouped, the main influences which are to impose themselves upon particular great agglomerations of new nationalities are the whole issue of the debate, and form the whole subject of this war.

The German Empire and its Ally, the Austro-Hungarian monarchy—that is, the reigning house of Hapsburg-Lorraine—wants the re-arrangement to take a certain form which would leave the German speech and culture and tradition the predominating thing in Europe, and probably in the whole world.

The Allies, upon the other hand, are fighting for a less simple idea. They are fighting for the double conception of:

> (*a*) Retaining the existing independence of certain national groups.
>
> (*b*) Erecting other independent or partly independent groups, the existence of which and the general influence of which shall restrict German and in particular Prussian power.

This dual conception the Allies rightly term the preservation and the extension of national liberties in Europe.

Now before we can comprehend either what the Germans are striving for or what the Allies are striving for, we must make a catalogue of those national groups which are at the foundation of the whole business. In making that catalogue we must remember what it is that creates a national group.

MAP I. THE MAIN TRUE NATIONAL FRONTIERS OF CONTINENTAL EUROPE
(excluding the South, which is exterior to this war)

▪ The Slavs Roman in Religion.   ▫ True National Frontiers.

1, 2, 3, 4.—Luxembourg, Belgium, Holland, Switzerland.

National groupings have discovered their power and have already begun to appear in real form through the artificial political boundaries which divided or suppressed them. Anyone proposing to reconstruct Europe must most certainly take account of such realities, and must deal with the many national groups of Europe as the stones out of which the new building is to be erected.

What makes a nation is *corporate tradition*. The strongest element in this is an historic memory. A nation which can point to having enjoyed a national existence in the past is much more firmly seated in its ambition to retain or to recover its independence than one which has never had such historic existence.

Another element in this constitution of a nationality is language. A common language is a much weaker element of nationality than tradition, as we see in the case of Belgium, which is almost equally divided between Latin-speaking and Teutonic-speaking people; and in the case of Switzerland. But it is none the less a strong thing; nowhere is it stronger than in the case of Poland. While, upon the other hand, you have exactly the opposite in the case of Irish national feeling; in the case of German-speaking Lorraine and Alsace; and you might very well have had a similar case in Bohemia where there is now a strong national feeling backed by a national Slav language, though that language was artificially revived comparatively recently.

Yet another factor is religion, and it is a most powerful one. It creates, for instance, a gulf between the Catholic and the Orthodox Slav, and it creates an awkward complexity in the problem of those Slavs whose religious ritual is Greek, but who are yet in communion with Rome.

It is impossible to attribute numerical value to each of these various factors, or to say that language everywhere counts for so much, religion for so much, etc. We have to take each particular case and judge it as it stands. And if we do that with an impartial judgment upon the real national feeling, we get some such list as the following, for the Continent alone.

(1) The French, who within their own boundaries are perfectly united; although certain districts (a little group in the Pyrenees and another little group in Western Brittany and another in the extreme north-east) speak a language of their own. To this French group should be added the provinces of Alsace and Lorraine which were annexed by the Germans in 1871. Alsace and Lorraine have enjoyed great material prosperity under German rule; the metal industry of the North has been immensely developed, and in a dozen other ways the German administration has increased their wealth, and has added to their population serious elements of German sympathy. But take the provinces as a whole and there is no doubt that their re-union with France is still the passionate desire of the great majority among them.

(2) Belgium is again undoubtedly the example of a separate—though less united—national group in whose individual feeling religion plays a great part, but still more historic existence through nearly a century as an independent State (during which century Belgium has vastly increased its population and its wealth), and for much more than a century the separate existence of the district as the Southern Netherlands as distinct from Holland.

(3) Holland, in its turn, both on account of its long independent existence, its strong national feeling and its peculiar experience as a commercial seafaring power, makes a third individual group. The populations immediately to the east of Holland in German territory speak a language of the same sort as the Dutch, and have the same social conditions and habits, but they have no desire to be Dutch, nor the Dutch to be incorporated with them.

(4) The Scandinavian countries, Denmark, Sweden, and Norway, form an equally distinct unit, and are quite clearly divided into three separate national groups. And here we have two anomalies: A quite small belt of Denmark, much smaller than the total original extent of Schleswig-Holstein, annexed by Prussia fifty years ago, is really Danish, and maintains to this day its protest against the annexation. One may go so far as to say that this really Danish belt is no more than a tenth of the whole, but its protest is a proof of the vigour which national feeling has maintained against artificial political boundaries. On the other hand, the Finnish provinces of Russia are, in their articulate spirit, their governing class, their religion, and almost in their entire social life Swedish in tone. Norway is intact, neither suffering a portion of her population under alien rule nor pretending to govern populations alien to herself.

(5) The fifth great group is the German, and here there is so much complexity that what we have to say must only be taken very generally and roughly. But, roughly and generally, the German group is as follows:

All German-speaking men and women with the exception of:

>   (*a*) The bulk of the annexed provinces of Alsace-Lorraine (a matter of sentiment), and

>   (*b*) The German-speaking cantons of Switzerland (a matter of political boundaries).

Now the boundaries of this "German feeling" group in Europe are curiously involved and tortuous. Beginning at the Baltic, roughly at the mouth of the River Niemen (which the Germans call the Memel), the true frontier of the German type runs southward for a short distance until it reaches what is called the Region of the Lakes, where the Russian frontier begins to turn west. There the boundary turns west also, and begins to run north again, nearly reaching the Baltic Sea in the neighbourhood of Dantzig. It then turns south by west, goes far west of Thorn and even of Posen, which are Polish towns, and comes round not far east of Frankfort-on-Oder. Then it goes south and east again, coming right through the middle of German Silesia, but, on reaching the mountains that here bound Bohemia, it curls round northwestward again, leaving the mountainous part of the barrier of Bohemia all German, but excluding the Slavonic true Bohemian people in the centre of that isolated region. The Upper Valley of the Elbe is not German. Having thus gone all the way round Bohemia proper, the boundaries of the German type run eastward again, very nearly following the watershed of the Danube until they strike the March River about thirty miles from Vienna. Vienna is thus not a centre, but, like Berlin, an outpost of German speech and civilization. From Vienna the true frontier of the German folk runs south, more or less corresponding to the existing boundary between Austria and Hungary, until it passes the point of Gratz—which counts as German. Thence the boundary turns due west again, taking in the greater part of the Tyrol, and so to the Swiss frontier and on to the Rhine opposite Belfort. Thence it follows the Rhine to a point south of Spiers, and after that follows the existing boundaries (excepting Luxembourg), and is confined by the Dutch and Belgian frontier and the North and Baltic Seas with the exception of the Danish belt north of the Kiel Canal, which is mainly Danish.

Within that curiously twisted line nearly all speech and all feeling is German. There are many States within that line, there is much confusion of historic tradition, a sharp division in religion—roughly Catholic in the south and west, Protestant in the north and east. But the national group is, especially as against the Slav and even as against western and southern Europe, one body; and within that body Prussia, with its capital of Berlin, is the organizing and directing centre.

Are there anomalies to be discovered with regard to this curiously shaped body? There are; but they are of less importance than is often imagined. Thus there are beyond Eastern Prussia and within the Russian boundary the so-called "German" Baltic provinces of Russia. But the term is a misnomer. The leaders of industry are largely German, most of the towns, and the greater landed aristocracy for the most part. But the mass of the population is not German-speaking, and even of the German-speaking minority only a minority again are in any sympathy with the united German feeling to the west.

There are colonies of German speech far eastward of Vienna under the political dominion of Hungary; a particularly large one being discoverable right up in the south-eastern Carpathians next to the Roumanian border. But these colonies could never be included in any united Germany. Nor could the considerable number of similar isolated colonies of Germans in southern and western Russia. Finally, you have on the extreme west the little province of Luxembourg, which is German-speaking, which has its railways and most of its industries controlled by Germans, but which would in any perfectly free system certainly refuse incorporation with any new German unity, for it has an historic tradition of independence which has proved very valuable to it, and may be compared with that of the Swiss German-speaking cantons.

(6) We next have to consider the Slavs, and these fall into two groups, northern and southern, which two groups are thus separated by the great Mongolian invasion of Eastern Europe in the Dark Ages. There is further among the Slavs a cross-section of great importance, that of religion. It separates the Slavs not into northern and southern, but, roughly, into eastern or Greek church, and western or Catholic. With the northern Slavs we count the Bohemians or Czechs, the Poles, and the Russians—using the latter term, of course, for many distinct but connected groups, for it is certain that Russia proper must remain a unity.

There are also just north of the Carpathians two minor northern Slavonic groups, the Slovacs and the Ruthenians. These northern Slavs are divided into Catholic Slavs and Slavs of the Greek Church, or Orthodox, by a vague belt of territory running, roughly, from the town of Vilna down to the borders of the Bukovina; the Poles and Czechs, etc., being in communion with Rome, while the Russians are of the Greek Church.

The southern Slavs are again divided into Catholic and Orthodox by a very sharp and bitter division. The Slovenes and the Croats stand for the Catholic group, the Serbian nation, as a whole, for the Orthodox group; a part of the Serbians and all the Slovenes and Croats are in the Austro-Hungarian dominions, and it is the Serbian element which is in rebellion. The rest of the Serbians are now independent. And so complicated are population and religion in this region that nearly a third of Bosnia and Herzegovina, while Slav in race, are Mohammedan in religion.

(7) Between these two great Slav groups, northern and southern, struck in, during the Dark Ages, a wedge of invading Mongols whose position has been of the greatest importance to the history of Eastern Europe. They were converted to Christianity nearly a thousand years ago, and the Mongol type has entirely disappeared, but the Mongol language remains under the title of *Magyar*, and it is the *Magyar*-speaking *Hungarians* that are the ruling race over all the eastern part of Austria-Hungary, though they are only half of the total population in their dominion. In any new national grouping this fiercely independent Magyar population must be taken for granted, though its claim to rule alien subjects is another matter.

(8) Finally, there is a curious group of the greatest importance, both because so much of its population is forbidden independence and because the remainder has attained independence. That group is the Roumanian group.

Racially, the Roumanians are probably Slavs for the most part, but their tongue is a Latin tongue; they are proud of Latin descent, and they are just as much a wedge between the Slavs of the north and south as the Magyars themselves. They everywhere overlap their nominal political boundaries; three million and a half of them extend far into Hungary, and a portion over the boundaries of Russia. For the most part they are Orthodox, or Greek, in religion. But it must always be remembered, because it is essential to understanding the new Europe, that the Roumanian-speaking people under Hungarian rule are, quite half of them and perhaps the majority, cut off from the Orthodox Church and in union with Rome.

With this summary, which has been expressed in Map I, you have a fair, though of course rough, division of Europe into its real national components.

Now let us ask what Germany and Austria would propose, in case of their victory, to make out of such materials.

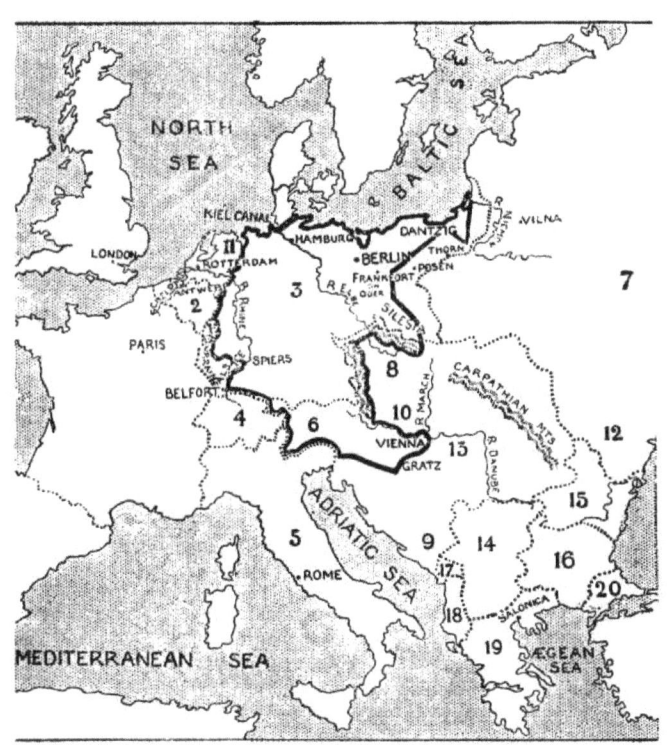

MAP II. THE GERMANIC GROUP IN EUROPE

1. Luxembourg	6. Mixed Italian and German	11. Holland	16. Bulgaria
2. Belgium	7. Russia	12. Bukovina	17. Montenegro
3. Germany	8. Bohemia	13. Hungary	18. Albania
4. Switzerland	9. Bosnia	14. Serbia	19. Greece
5. Italy	10. Austrian	15. Roumania	20. Turkey

The boundaries of the "German feeling" group in Europe are very roughly suggested by the thick black line. Within that curiously twisted line nearly all speech and all feeling is German.

In the first place Germany would keep all that she has, indifferent to national anomalies or the unquiet of subject and oppressed peoples. She would keep Alsace-Lorraine; she would keep in subjection the Poles who are already in subjection to her; she would leave the Austro-Hungarian Monarchy under the Hapsburgs with all its present possessions, whether those possessions grossly interfered with national realities or no. Would she annex territory, in spite of the first of the two postulates which I have already mentioned?

The German constitutional system is of its nature federal. There is room in it for many kinds of states, each possessed of a very great measure of independence, and if the inclusion within one commercial system and one military system also, however loose that inclusion, be called annexation, then we may say that Germany would annex in some degree. She would wish to control directly the Mouth of the Scheldt and probably the Teutonic-speaking part of Belgium, that is, the north of that country. She would certainly desire to administer the Ardennes, which would be her frontier against France, and she would quite certainly take over Luxembourg.

As to Holland, her plan would probably be different there from that pursued in any other case. She would leave it as independent in its own eyes as it was before; she might insist upon an alliance with the Dutch army, she would certainly insist upon commercial terms, and probably rights of using certain ports in certain cases for war. But nothing but inexcusable folly would tempt her to go further. The position of Holland after a German settlement might not uncertainly be compared to the position of Hamburg in the old days, on a larger scale, a free State just as Hamburg was a free city.

This easy and, as it were, mutually arranged compromise with Holland, coupled with dominion over the Scheldt and Antwerp, would give the German peoples what they most desire, the whole littoral of the North Sea. Further, possessing Antwerp, as they would certainly possess it, they would have a commercial lever for keeping Holland in order. They could direct all their trade at will towards Antwerp to the starvation of Rotterdam.

The Scandinavian countries they would regard as naturally German in feeling, and as falling in a vague and general way into their orbit. Possessing the Kiel Canal, they would not strictly need the Sound. But they would so dominate Denmark that they could make what commercial or military terms they chose with regard to the passages of the Baltic; and you would have German firms, German methods, and to some extent the German language holding "civil garrisons" throughout the useful part of Sweden and Norway.

On the East some have imagined they would erect as against Russia a mutilated and dependent Polish State. It is more probable that they would confine themselves to procuring some liberty for Russian Poland, and obtaining some convention as to fortification and commerce. Russia will always be formidable, and to maintain the mutual bond of a subject Poland between Russia and herself would serve in the future, as it has served in the past, the ends of Prussia. It is essential to Prussia that no really independent Poland should re-arise, even mutilated. It is even essential that there should be no one area that the Poles could regard as the nucleus of a really free Polish State.

In the Balkans the Germanic Powers would certainly demand the control over what is now Serbia, and, at the risk of further war, the outlet at Salonika. The remnant of the Turkish Empire in Europe they already regard as being under their protectorate.

As to the West, they would, rightly, treat it merely as a defeated foe. France (they would say) might continue to decline—for the Germans, getting things out of Berlin, always talk of "the decay of the Latin peoples"—her decline accelerated by stringent commercial treaties and a heavy indemnity; England would be envisaged in the same terms. Germany would demand from England certain coaling stations; she would impose on England also certain commercial conditions. But there would be no need to restrict the building of a Fleet, for there a victorious Germany would feel easily able to look after herself.

MAP III. EUROPE REMODELLED BY GERMANY AND AUSTRIA

Boundary of Germanic Allies to-day, with their dependent States.

Small districts which might be actually annexed: the Lower Scheldt, Middle Meuse, Ardennes, Luxembourg, a corner of French Lorraine, a few frontier districts of Russian Poland.

Countries which would be dependent upon the Germanic hegemony, being of kindred blood and speech, and which would in special points admit actual economic or political control by Germans.

Holland, a special case. Kindred in speech. Not actually annexed, perhaps, but allowed only a quasi-independent position with German control, veiled, in the two principal ports, and facilities for German Navy. Also included in any economic policy.

Districts in no way kindred to Germanic peoples, but to be annexed, or at any rate directly controlled in order to command the Balkans, to dominate Constantinople, and to get a passage to the Ægean Sea.

Buffer Polish States, which Prussia might erect dependent on herself and as a barrier against Russia.

District which German Empire might annex, both on account of its German elements in population, and on account of controlling the Baltic.

One may sum up and say that Germany and Austria expect from victory a Europe in which all that is German-speaking and already within their moral influence shall support their power over the world, that power not coming in the shape of annexations, save at one or two selected points.

Once on the North Sea, and once having broken British maritime supremacy, Central Europe would leave the future to do its work, content in the East with dominating the Balkans and reaching the Ægean Sea, and with permanently holding back the further advance of Russia.

MAP IV. EUROPE REMODELLED BY THE ALLIES

1. To retain their present boundaries: Switzerland, Belgium, Luxembourg, Holland, Norway, Sweden.

2. The Germanic Peoples: with the Catholic South leaning upon Vienna and a large autonomy to individual States.

3. France: with Alsace-Lorraine.

4. Poland: Quasi-independent, but a holding of Russia.

5. Czechs: Quasi-independent, but probably still a holding of Vienna.

6. Ruthenians (a minor Slavonic group): either annexed to Russia, or closely dependent on her.

7. An independent Magyar State.

8. An independent Catholic Southern Slav or Croat State, probably a holding of Vienna.

9. An orthodox Southern Slav State, Serbia, with access to Adriatic, but not holding Bulgarian territory.

10. Roumania, enlarged by her Transylvanian population.

11. Bulgaria.

If this is the German programme, what is that of the Allies?

Primarily, it is the maintenance of not only liberties, but powers already acquired. In the economic sphere it is, of course, the maintenance of those international contracts upon which the wealth of England and of France depends. It is the maintenance of English power at sea, the re-establishment of a united France by land, the recovery of Belgium, and the guaranteeing of Holland in her neutrality, whether she wills it or no.

But over and beyond this there is the problem of reconstruction, and here you have two clear principles:

(1) It is to the advantage of the Allies to recognize everywhere, as much as possible, the realities of nationality.

(2) It is a matter of life and death to the Allies to prevent the re-establishment of Prussian power, with its ideal of domination over others.

To some extent these two policies agree, but not entirely. To erect a larger Serbia, to free the Croats and the Slovenes, or perhaps to take from their territory the ports necessary to Serbia on the Adriatic, giving Serbia also the territory of Bosnia and Herzegovina; meanwhile, to let Bulgaria occupy the purely Bulgarian districts which Serbia now has, to re-erect a united Poland, to give Roumania her nationals beyond the Carpathians at the expense of Hungary; to make Hungary as far as possible independent of Vienna in administration, and in particular in military affairs—all that is part of universal policy which everyone expects.

But what of Germany from within?

It is evident that the control of the Baltic, which the Kiel Canal involves, means that the Kiel Canal should be neutralized. It is equally evident that, while the Bohemians may not be wholly separated from the Germanic body which nearly encloses them, the largest measure of autonomy for these isolated Slavs fits the case of the Allies. But as for the policy to be pursued for Germany herself in case of a victory on the part of the Allies, that is a much more complex matter.

Roughly, it would seem to depend upon two main principles: First, that the more ancient and the more civilized pole of Germany, the southern pole which is at Vienna, should be in every way favoured at the expense of the northern pole, Berlin, to which we have owed this catastrophe. Secondly, that an economic policy should be imposed which shall leave industrial Germany free to produce and yet compelled to pay.

A policy of that kind means, of course, a carefully framed tariff, so designed that the tribute necessary to paying the cost of this great adventure shall fall upon its authors.

Germany showed the way in 1871 upon what now looks like a modest scale, but was then designed to be ruthless. It is our business to copy that example.

NUMBERS IN WAR

In which it is explained why, other things being equal, numbers are always the deciding element in warfare, and how the enemy had a superiority throughout the autumn and winter (written late in the winter of 1914-1915).

NUMBERS IN WAR

THE general reader hears continually in these times that *numbers* are the decisive element in war. That every authority, every student and every soldier is convinced of it, he cannot fail to see from the nature of the orders given and of the appeals made. Numbers in material, and in men, are the one thing urged. The public critique of the war is filled with estimates of enemy and allied numbers, numbers of reserve, numbers of killed, numbers of prisoners. The whole of the recruiting movement in this country is based on this same conception of numbers.

Now the general reader may appreciate the general character of this conception, but he must often be puzzled by the detailed application of it.

If I am told that ten men are going to fight eight, the mere sound of the figures suggests superiority on the part of the ten, but unless I know how they are going to fight, I should be puzzled to say exactly how the extra two would tell. I certainly could not say whether the two would be enough to make a serious difference or not, and I might come to a very wrong conclusion about the chances of the eight or the ten. So it is worth while if one is attempting to form a sound opinion upon the present campaign to see exactly how and why numbers are the deciding factor in war.

In the first place it is evident that numbers only begin to tell when other things are fairly equal. Quite a few men armed with rifles will be a match for multitudes deprived of firearms, and the history of war is full of smaller forces defeating larger forces from Marathon to Ligny. But when war follows upon a long period of peace and takes place between nations of one civilization all closely communicating one with another, and when war has been the principal study of those nations during the period of peace, then all elements except those of numbers do become fairly equal. And that is exactly the condition of the present campaigns.

The enemy have certain advantages in material, or had at the beginning of the struggle, notably in the matter of heavy artillery, but much more in the accurate forecast they had made of the way in which modern fighting would turn. All sorts of their tactical theories turned out to be just.

The Allied forces had advantages—the English in personal equipment, medical and commissariat service; the French, Russians, and Serbians, in the type of field gun. The French in particular in their theory of strategy, which has proved sound.

But there was no conspicuous difference such as would make a smaller number able to defeat a much larger one, and the historical observer at a distance of time that will make him impartial, will certainly regard the war as one fought between forces of nearly the same weaponing and training. The one great differentiating point will be numbers.

Now how is it that these numbers tell?

There are two aspects of the thing which I will call (1) The Effect of *Absolute* Numbers and (2) The Effect of *Proportionate* Numbers.

(1) *Absolute Numbers*. I mean by the effect of absolute numbers the fact that a certain minimum is required for any particular operation. For instance, if you were holding a wall a mile long which an enemy upon the other side desired to surmount, it is evident that you could not hold such a wall with one man even though the enemy on the other side consisted only in one man. The opportunities for the success of the enemy would be too great. You could not hold it with ten men against ten. You could hardly hold it with 100 men against 100. But supposing that you have 3000 men to hold it with, and they are using no weapons save their hands, then 3000 men could hold the wall not only against 3000 others, but against any number of thousands of others; for every man would have as his task the pushing of a ladder off no more than a very small section of the wall with which his own hands could deal.

There we see what is meant by the necessity of absolute numbers or a minimum.

Now that is exactly what you have in the case of a great line of trenches. Your defending force does not get weaker and weaker as it diminishes in number until it reaches zero; it is able to hold trenches of a certain length with a certain minimum of men, and when it falls below that minimum *it cannot hold the line at all*. It has to fall back upon a shorter line. Supposing you have, for instance, under such conditions as those of Diagram I, a line of trenches A-B holding the issue between two obstacles X and Y against an enemy who attacks from the direction E. The number of men holding these trenches, A-B, is nine units, and this number is just enough, and only just enough, to prevent an enemy attacking from E getting through. Nine units just prevent any part of the line of trenches, A-B, from being left defenceless.

What does one mean by saying: "Just enough to prevent an enemy getting through?"

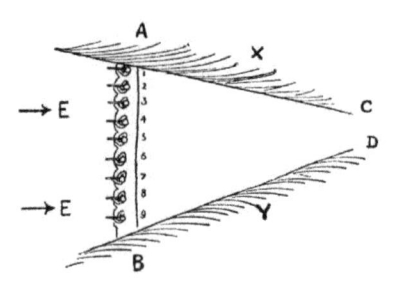

DIAGRAM I. Suppose you have a line of trenches A-B holding the issue between two obstacles X and Y against an enemy who attacks from the direction E. The number of men holding those trenches is nine units, and this number is only just enough to prevent the attacking force getting through.

One means that if you consider trenches in detail, a certain length of trench needs a certain number of men to hold it, and if that number of men is not present, it must be altogether abandoned. It is evident that a mile of trench, for instance, could not be held by half-a-dozen men, even if the forces opposed to them were only a half-dozen.

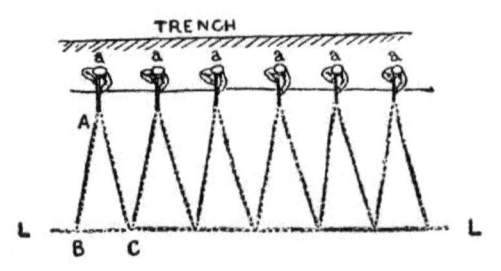

DIAGRAM II. Every man in a trench may be regarded as accounting for a certain angle of space in front of him, as A-B-C. If the extreme point at which you can stop a rush is the line L-L then you must have at least enough men—a-a-a—to cover that line with their fire.

You must, first, have enough men to cover the field of fire in front of the trench with the missiles from the weapons of each, and so stop the assault of the enemy. Every man with his rifle may be regarded as accounting for a certain angle of space in front of him as in the angles A B C and the other similar angles in Diagram II. These angles must meet and cover the whole ground, in theory at least, not further from the trench than the most advanced point to which it has been discovered that an enemy's rush will reach before combined fire stops it. In practice, of course, you need very many more men, but the theory of the thing is that if the extreme point at which you can expect to stop a rush is the line L-L, and if the angle over which a rifle is usefully used is the angle B-A-C, then you cannot hold the trench at all unless you have at least enough men a-a-a just to cover that line L-L with their fire. If you try to do it with less men, as in Diagram III, you would only cover a portion of the front; you would leave a gap in it between X and Y through which the trench would be carried.

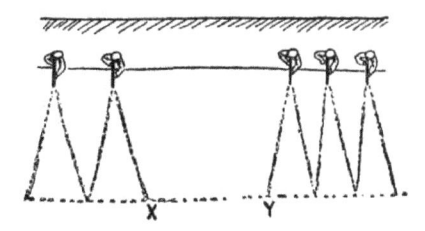

DIAGRAM III. If you try to hold your trench with less men, as in this diagram, you would only cover a portion of the front; you would leave a gap in it, between X and Y, through which the trench would be carried.

It is evident, I repeat, that in practice there are needed to hold trenches a great many more men than this. You must allow for your wastage, for the difference in ability and coolness of different men, for the relieving of the men at regular and fairly short intervals, and in general, it will be found that a line of trenches is not successfully held with less than 3000 men to a mile.

The Germans are now holding in the West a line of trenches 500 miles long with something like 4000 men to a mile; so the best work in the war would seem to have been done by a portion of the British contingent in front of Ypres when, apparently, a body only 1500 men to the mile, and those I understand, dismounted cavalry, successfully held some three miles of trenches for several days.

It is apparent, then, that when you are considering a line of trenches you must consider them as a series of sections, to defend each of which sections a certain minimum is required. Thus we may consider the line A-B in Diagram IV as consisting of nine sections, as numbered, and each section as requiring a certain minimum unit of men, say a thousand. If any section has less than its proper minimum the whole line fails, for that section will be carried and the cord will be broken.

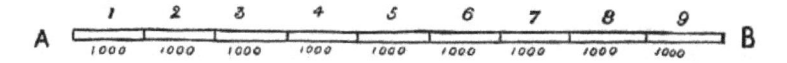

DIAGRAM IV. The line of trenches A-B may consist of nine sections, to defend each of which 1000 men are required. If any section has less than its proper minimum the whole line fails.

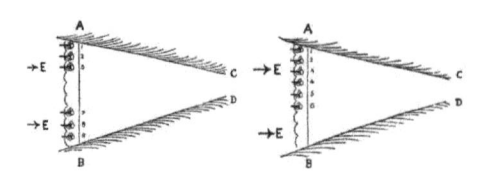

DIAGRAMS V and VI. Suppose by killed, wounded and prisoners the nine sections dwindle to six, the line A-B can no longer be held. The six remaining sections would have to group themselves as above, and in either case there would be a bad gap. What then can the general in command of this dwindled force do?—

(See Diagram VII overleaf.)

Now look back at the first diagram; there you have the line A-B, and there are nine units just able to hold it.

Suppose by killed and prisoners and wounded and disease the nine dwindle to six, then the line A-B can no longer be held. It means in practice that the six remaining would have to be grouped as in Diagram V or as in Diagram VI, and in any case there would be a bad gap, double or single, through which the enemy pressing from E would pierce. What can the general in command of the defence do when his force has thus dwindled?

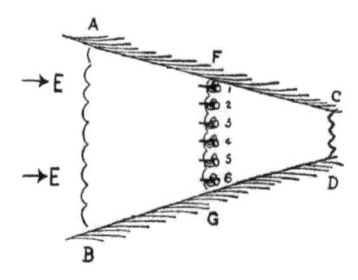

DIAGRAM VII. The defender has no choice but to fall back on shorter lines, such as F-G, which his remaining six units can just hold. If the six dwindle to four he must again fall back to a yet shorter line, C-D.

He has no choice but to *fall back upon shorter lines*. That is, having only six units left he must retire to some such point as the line F-G, Diagram VII, where his remaining six units will be just sufficient to hold the line, and if the six dwindle to four he must again fall back to a yet shorter line, such as C-D.

Note carefully that this does not concern proportionate numbers. We are not here considering the relative strength of the defence and of the offence; we are dealing with absolute numbers, with a minimum below which the defensive *cannot* hold a certain line at all, but *must* seek a shorter one.

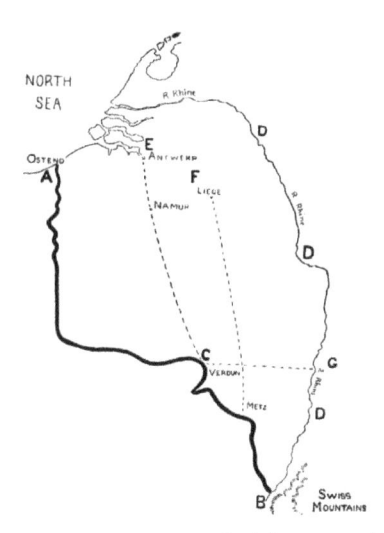

DIAGRAM VIII. The Germans are now holding, roughly, the line A-B, from the North Sea to the Swiss Mountains—500 miles long in all its twists and turns. If dwindling numbers force them to take up a shorter line they could either abandon Alsace-Lorraine and substitute C-G for C-B, or abandon most of Belgium and Northern France and substitute E-C for A-C. With still failing numbers they would have to take up the still shorter line F-B. It would be no shortening of the German line to fall back upon the Rhine, D-D-D.

Now that is precisely the state of affairs upon the French and Belgian frontiers at this moment. The Germans are holding a line, which is roughly that shown in Diagram VIII, between the Swiss mountains and the sea near Nieuport, the line A-B about 400 miles long in all its twists and turns. If their numbers fall below a certain level they cannot hold that line at all, and they must take up a shorter line. How could they do this? Either by abandoning Alsace-Lorraine and substituting C-G for the present C-B, or by abandoning most of Belgium and all northern France, and falling back upon the line Antwerp-Namur-The Ardennes and the Vosges, substituting E-C for A-C. With failing numbers they would have to take up a still shorter line from Liege southwards, just protecting German territory, the line F-B.

As for the line of the Rhine lying immediately behind F-B, the line D-D-D, it is a great deal longer than the shortest line they could take up. F-B, and though heavily fortified at five important points and with slighter fortifications elsewhere, it would need quite as many men to defend it as a corresponding line of trenches. Thus it would be no shortening of the German line to fall back upon the Rhine.

So much for an illustration of what is meant by absolute numbers and of their importance in the present phase of the campaign.

(2) Now what of *Proportionate* numbers? That is a point upon which even closer attention must be fixed, because upon it will depend the issue of the campaign.

The first thing we have to see clearly is that Austria and Germany began the war with a very great preponderance in numbers of trained and equipped men ready to take the field within the first six weeks. They had here a great advantage over Russia and France combined, and to see what that advantage was look at Diagram IX.

A
B   C
FRANCE   GERMANY   RUSSIA

DIAGRAM IX. A represents the total number of men Germany and Austria together could put into the field by about the middle of September. B represents the French and the first British contingent; C what the Russians could do. This shows that Germany and Austria began the war with a great advantage over Russia, France and Britain combined, in their numbers of trained and equipped men ready to take the field within the first six weeks.

Figure A represents the total number of men Germany and Austria together could put into the field by about the middle of September. B represents the French and the first British contingent in the West; C what the Russians could do in the East.

This original superiority of the enemy is a point very little appreciated because of two things. First, that men tend to think of the thing in nations and not in numbers, and they think of Germany, one unit, attacked by England, France, Russia, a lot of other units, and next because there is a grave misconception as to the numbers Russia could put into the field *early* in the war.

Russia had a certain force quite ready, that is fully equipped, officered, trained, gunned, and the rest of it. But she had nothing like the numbers in proportion to her population that the enemy had. The proportions of population were between Russia and her enemy as seventeen to thirteen. But

Germany and, to a less extent, Austria and Hungary, had organized the whole population ultimately for war. Russia could not do this. Her advantage, only to be obtained after a considerable lapse of time, was the power of perpetually raising new contingents, which, by the time they were trained and equipped could successively enter the field. But at the opening of the war, say by the middle of September, when she had perhaps at the most two-and-a-half million men in Poland, the total forces of the enemy, that is the total number of men Austria and Germany had equipped, trained, and ready for the field since the beginning of the war, was at least eight million.

You have the war, then, beginning with the enemy standing at quite 8, the French nominally at 4, but really nearer 3; Russia at 2½.

Let us see how time was to modify this grave disproportion and how new contingents coupled with the effect of wastage were to affect it.

The armies which were in the field in the early part of the war bear very various relations to the countries from which they come.

Great Britain had upon the Sambre in the first battle of the campaign rather more than one-tenth per cent. of her total population. The French had in the field at the outset of the war 5 per cent. of their total population, the Russians 1 per cent., the Germans perhaps 5 per cent., the Austrians between 3 and 4 per cent., the Serbians quite 10 per cent.—and 10 per cent. is the largest total any nation can possibly put into the field.

Now the chances of growth for each of these contingents were very different in each case.

That of Great Britain was indefinitely large. Given sufficient time, sufficient money, and sufficient incentive, Great Britain might ultimately put into the field two million or even three. She was certain of putting into the field in the first year of the war more than one million; she might hope to put in two. She had further behind her as a recruiting field, the Colonies, and—a matter of discussion—the Indian Army.

The French had nothing to fall back on save the young men who were growing up. Therefore, they were certain not to be able to add to their numbers for at least six months, which is just about the time it takes to train effectively new formations.

The Germans had in reserve about as many men again as they had put under arms at the beginning of the war. If the French could hope for a grand total of four millions wherein somewhat over three might be really effective and of useful age for active service in any shape, then Germany might hope to produce a grand total of somewhat over seven millions and a similar useful body of over five, for the German adult males are to the French as more than five to three.

Austria could in the same way call up a reserve somewhat larger in proportion than the Germans, but as her population was somewhat smaller than Germany, we must write her down for something over four millions instead of something over five, for a grand total of between five and six millions instead of for a grand total of seven.

Serbia, like France, could not increase her contingent save by calling up her younger men; and her army was, like that of the French, a fixed quantity, at any rate for the first six months of the war, and increased by one-tenth or less when the new class was trained.

Russia in her turn presented yet another type of growth. She had by far larger reserves of adult males than any other Power, and was practically equal, in the material of which one can ultimately make trained soldiers, to Germany and Austria combined; theoretically, counting all her various races, she was the superior of Austria and Germany combined. But it was certain that she could not equip more than a certain number in a given time, or train them, or officer them, or govern them.

I think it just to say that she certainly could not put into the European field more than five millions during the better part of the first year of the war. Though it must be remembered that if the war lasted indefinitely she would have at her back at any period indefinitely large reserves to draw upon.

Let us call Russia ultimately, for the purposes of the war during all its first months, a minimum of three and a maximum of five millions. Let us count Great Britain in those same months at two millions, including all who have gone out, all since recruited, and the many more who will not be either recruited or fully trained for some months to come—but excluding foreign garrisons and naval forces. Such an estimate is certainly a maximum for that period.

Then putting all these figures together and considering for the moment no wastage, the figures become as in Diagram X.

                    A
        B   C

            FRANCE   GERMANY   RUSSIA

DIAGRAM X. How will time modify the grave disproportion indicated in Diagram IX? Taking, roughly, the first few months of the war, apart from wastage, our enemies remain month after month far superior to either half of the Allies they are fighting—the French and English in the West, the Russians in the East.

Observe in this diagram and retain it for purposes of judgment throughout the war—it is far the most important truth to retain—that, apart from wastage, our enemies remained throughout the winter far superior to either half of the Allies they are fighting. Remember that we did not put as against Austro-Germany in the West more than 6 to 9 for a long time, nor Russia in the East certainly more than 5 to 9.

The Allies combined will at last be superior to their enemy numerically, but only superior in a proportion of 11 to 9 (exclusive of wastage), and that maximum will not be reached till summer.

I have italicized that paragraph because the misapprehension of so simple a truth is at the bottom of three-quarters of the nonsense one hears about the campaign. It was at the bottom of the conception that victory would be easy and short; at the bottom of the conception that it would be certain, and it is at the bottom of much foolish impatience and criticism to-day.

It was a knowledge of this truth which made the German Government feel secure of success when it forced on the war at its chosen day and hour (remember with what curious superstition the Germans passed the frontier on the same day and at the same hour as in 1870), and an ignorance of it alone can account for the follies one still hears.

Even as I write I rise from reading the account of a sermon by some clergyman, an Englishman—but not in England, I am glad to say—who talked of Germany, with her back to the wall, fighting the world, and expressing his admiration thereat. He had evidently never considered the element of numbers.

Now what about the wastage?

Luckily for us, German necessities, as well as German doctrine, have involved very heavy wastage. And, luckily for us, that wastage has been particularly heavy in the matter of officers.

A discussion on numbers does not allow one to stray into the equally important moral factors of the war, but the fact may be just alluded to that the whole general military organism of Germany depends more than that of any other nation upon the gulf between the officer and those next in command. Not only can you make a French non-commissioned officer into an officer without fear of losing an atom of the moral strength of the French military organism, but the thing is done continually during peace and during war on a large scale. In Germany you can do nothing of the kind.

The attack in close formation, with all its obvious advantages of speed and with all the very fine tradition of discipline which makes it possible, is another element of expense, but most expensive of all is the determination to win at once.

Why have the Germans been thus prodigal of men in their determination to win rapidly? A long war is dreaded by Germany for four separate and equal reasons:

> (1) That in a really considerable length of time two of her opponents are capable of indefinite expansion—Russia and Great Britain.
>
> (2) Because all historical experience is there to show that the French are a nation that rally, and that unless you pin them after their first defeats their tenacity will be increasingly dangerous.
>
> (3) Because the power of the British Fleet is capable of establishing a blockade more or less complete, and hitherto only less complete from political considerations.
>
> (4) Because the strategical problem, the fighting upon two fronts, involves, as a method of victory, final success upon one front before you can be certain of success upon the other.

This last point merits illustration. An army fighting inferior bodies on two fronts is just like a very big man fighting two much smaller men. They can harass him more than their mere fighting power or weight accounts for, and they can do so because they are attacking upon different sides.

The big man so situated will certainly attempt to put out of action one of his two opponents before he puts his full force against the other. It would be a plan necessary to the situation, and it is exactly the same with a Power or a group of Powers fighting upon two fronts, although they find themselves in superior numbers on either front, as the Austro-Germans do still.

For all these four reasons, then, Germany was bound to waste men, and she did waste men largely until about the end of last year. She threw them away recklessly during the first advance on Paris, next during the great attacks in Flanders, then—quite separately—in her desperate Polish effort to reach Warsaw, which goal, at the moment of writing, she has wholly failed to attain.

But though we know that Germany and Austro-Hungary have lost men in a greater proportion than the Western Allies, and though we may guess that they have lost men in a greater proportion than our Eastern Allies—in spite of the heavy losses in prisoners at Tannenberg—it is less easy to give an accurate estimate of the proportion.

In one case and up to one date we can arrive pretty accurately at the proportion. The German Empire alone had, up to a particular date in the autumn, lost in hit, sick, and caught (I will speak in a moment of the question of "returns") 40 per cent. of the individuals up to that date put into the field. Both the French and the English had up to the same date lost just under 25 per cent.

I know that that figure 40 per cent. looks absurdly exaggerated when it is put thus without support, but it is a perfectly sound conclusion. If you take the lists published by Prussia, note the dates to which they refer, the proportion of killed to the *admitted* wounded, and add the proportion for Bavaria, Wurtemburg, and Saxony, you find that at this date in the late autumn two millions were affected, and Germany had not armed more than five millions at the most at that time.

Now, as in our own case, the proportion of officers hit, wounded, and caught was large compared to that of men; but what is more important, perhaps, the proportion of officers killed or badly wounded was very much larger in proportion to the slightly wounded than was the case with the men; it is fairly certain that one-half of the trained professional officers of the German service were permanently out of action by the end of the year.

Supposing the Russian losses to be no greater than the Western Allies (they probably are somewhat greater, from the conditions of the fighting), or call them 30 per cent. instead of 25 per cent., and supposing the Austro-Hungarian losses to be comparable to the German (which, from the only available sources of statistics, they would seem to be), then we can strike a very rough estimate of the element of wastage, and we can say that if the central figure be taken as 9, 3.6 have gone; while of the 4 and 3 on either side (the proportionate strength of the Allies West and East in the first phase) 1 has gone in each case, leaving 3 and 2.

It will be seen that, from this rough calculation, the wastage of the enemy has been so much greater than our own that, if it were absolute, his preponderance in numbers would have ceased, and the figures would stand nearly equal.

But there is one last element in the calculation which must not be forgotten. The only people permanently out of action in the war are the killed, the disabled, and the captured. Much the greater part of the sick return to the centre, and *just over half the wounded*—at least, in a modern war, and where there are good ambulance arrangements and good roads for them to work on.

Now, though these "returns" are probably smaller in the East than in the West (for in the Eastern field climate and absence of communication are fatal to many of the wounded, who would be saved in the Western field), we should do well to take a conservative estimate, and regard it as half the wounded in each case; or, excluding prisoners, more than a third—say, 35 per cent. of all casualties.

We must add, therefore, in that proportion to all our figures, and the result will slightly modify our conclusion, for as the central body—the enemy—has had more casualties, so it has a larger number of returns in proportion to its size, and the general deduction is that at the moment of writing (late winter) the Germanic body and the Allies opposed to them actually in the field or in training—just behind the field and ready to approach it within a few weeks—are nearly equal in total numbers, but with an appreciable margin still in favour of the enemy.

SUPPLY

After numbers, the second main factor in the strength of an army is its supply—its means of obtaining clothes, food, shelter, ammunition and all those objects without which it can neither exist nor fight. The marvellously complicated and expensive organization entailed is here fully explained.

SUPPLY

AN army has two main factors of strength—that is, two main material factors apart from the moral factors of courage, discipline, habit, and relationship. These two material factors are first its numbers, and secondly its supply.

The first of these is so much the more obvious in the public eye that it is often alone considered. It is, of course, the basis of all the rest. Unless you have a sufficient number of men for your task you cannot accomplish that task at all. But the second, which is less often considered by general opinion, is a necessity no less absolute than the necessity for adequate numbers.

The general term "supply" covers all those objects without which an army cannot exist or fight—clothing, shelter, food, weapons, auxiliary instruments, ammunition.

Now it is not the intention of these few lines to enter into details or to give precise information, such as may be obtained by reference to the text books, but rather to bring out a few main points about supply which are not generally considered, especially in moments such as this, when the obtaining of numbers by voluntary recruitment is the chief matter in the public mind. And these chief points with regard to supply may be put briefly in three groups.

First we ought to grasp the *scale* of supply: that is, the magnitude of the operation which is undertaken when an army is equipped, put into the field, and maintained there.

Next we must grasp the *rate* of supply—the pace at which the stream of supply has got to be kept moving (varying for various forms of supply) in order that an army shall neither break down nor dwindle in efficiency.

Lastly we must consider the *delicacy* or liability to *embarrassment* of supply; that is, the difficulties peculiar to the maintenance of an army in the field, the ease with which that maintenance may be fatally interrupted, and the consequent embarrassment which an enemy may be made to feel, or which the enemy may make us feel, in this vital operation of war.

As to the scale of supply. Remark that there are in this factor a number of elements easily overlooked, and the first is the element of comparative expense. It is of no great value to put before men rows of figures showing that a large army costs so many millions of pounds. It is the *comparative* economic burden of armed service as contrasted with civilian work which is really of importance, and which is much more easily grasped than the absolute amount of the cost.

The great mass of men in an army are, of course, drawn from the same rank of society as the great mass of labourers and artisans during peace, and the very first point we have to note about a state of war is that these men are provided for their trade with instruments and provisions upon a higher scale than anything which they require in their civilian life.

DIAGRAM I. The great mass of men in the army are drawn from the same rank of society as the great mass of labourers and artisans during peace; but they are provided for their trade with instruments and provisions upon a higher scale than anything which they required in their civilian life. The difference in the cost of upkeep—clothing, food, implements, etc.—of a navvy and a soldier for one year is shown approximately in the above diagram.

Their clothing is and must be better, for the wear of a campaign is something very different from the wear of ordinary living. It is to this factor that one owes not a little of the complaints that always arise during a war upon the quality of the material used by contractors.

Let me give an example drawn from my personal experience. If I am not mistaken, the heavy dark blue great-coat worn by the gunners in the French service costs (when all expense was reduced to a minimum through the agency of Government factories, through the purchase of clothing wholesale, and through the absence of a whole series of those profits attaching to ordinary trade) no less than 100 francs, or £4. That great-coat stood for material and workmanship which, sold in a West End shop in London, would have meant anything from £6 upwards. In other words, the private soldiers all through a vast body of men were wearing a great-coat of a quality—in expense, at least—which only very well-to-do men, only a tiny minority in the State, could afford in time of peace.

Next observe that you feed the man (I am glad to say) far better than the modern capitalist system of production feeds him. You must do this, or you would not be able to maintain your army at its highest efficiency.

Many a man who in civilian life would never get butcher's meat more than once or twice a week, receives a pound and a quarter of meat a day in an army. He receives over a pound of bread. And it is curious to note in a conscript service how small a proportion of the men—only those, indeed, who are drawn from quite the wealthier classes—find the provisioning of the army distasteful (none find it inadequate), and how, for the great majority, it is an advance over that to which they were accustomed at home.

But there is much more than this high scale of expenditure in the things necessary to the maintenance of the man himself. You are also equipping him with special furniture far more expensive than that which he uses in ordinary life.

You give to the minesman a rifle which is a carefully constructed and expensive machine, much more valuable than all the tools that would ever be in the possession of any but a small minority of skilled artisans. He has belt, pouches, pack covering to match. He must expend in the use of that weapon ammunition costing something quite out of proportion to any expenditure involved by the use of his implements in his civilian trade.

The cavalryman you equip with a horse, which he could not think of affording as his own property, and which is superior in quality to the horse he may be working with for a master in most trades, let alone the fact that the proportion of men thus equipped with horses is much larger than the proportion of men who in civilian life have to deal with those animals. To the driver of a gun you are apportioning two horses necessarily sound and strong; to the non-commissioned officers throughout the field artillery, to a great number of officers throughout the service, you are furnishing horses which, in a civilian occupation, they could never afford, and you are, of course, also providing the keep of those horses.

Many branches of the service you are equipping with instruments of very high expense indeed. A field gun does not cost less, I believe, than £600. And to every thousand men you actually put into the field you may reckon at least four of these instruments. Every time one of them fires a shot it fires away fifteen shillings. Apart from the wear and tear of the field piece itself, a modern quick-firing piece, firing moderately, will get rid of a ten pound note in ammunition in a minute, and each piece is allowed from the base onwards 1000 rounds.

Further, an army is equipped with heavy artillery, the pieces of which cost anything from many hundreds to many thousands of pounds, according to their calibre (a 9.2, with its mounting, comes to near £12,000); and it is also equipped with a mass of auxiliary material—vehicles, mechanical and other, telephones, field kitchens, aircraft, and the rest—none of which expense attaches to the same body of men in their civilian life.

The scale of the business is further emphasised by the fact that once war is engaged the nation as a whole is suddenly called upon to produce material not only *more expensive* upon the average, man for man, than the same men would have used and consumed in the same time in civilian life, but things *different from* those things which the nation was organized to produce for use and consumption during peace. That change in effect is costly. And yet another element of cost is the novel use of existing instruments.

DIAGRAM II. Many branches of the service are equipped with instruments of very high expense indeed. A field gun, for instance, does not cost less than £600. Every time one of them fires a shot it fires away fifteen shillings. A modern quick-firing piece, firing moderately, will get rid of a ten pound note in ammunition in a minute. Each piece is allowed from the base onwards 1000 rounds and the extent of this quantity is illustrated in the diagram—40 rows of shells, 25 in a row.

It is more expensive to use an instrument for some purpose for which it was never designed, than to use it for some purpose for which it was designed. That is a universal truth from the hammering in of a nail with a boot heel to the commandeering of a liner for the transport of troops. And in time of war the whole nation begins at once to use instruments right and left for military purposes, which instruments had been originally designed for civilian purposes.

All up and down France and England, for instance, at this moment, every workshop which can by hook or by crook turn out ammunition is turning it out, and very often is turning it out with instruments—lathes, cutting tools, etc.—that were originally designed not for making ammunition at all, but for making the parts of bicycles, of pumps, of motors, of turbines, etc.

Another instance. Both Powers have found their motor-buses extremely handy in this war. Paris has been almost bereft of them. London has been largely denuded of her normal supply. But a motor-bus carrying meat or even troops is not doing what it was specially designed to do—to wit, to run on the good roads of a great town, with a certain maximum load. It needs adaptation, it is used far more roughly, has a shorter life, and is being therefore more expensively consumed.

Here is one fairly graphic way of showing what this scale of supply means. Take an Army Corps of 40,000 men. That stands in meat alone for one year for about as many beasts. It means in clothing alone—initial expense—apart from waste of all kinds, and apart from weapons and auxiliary machinery, something between (counting accoutrement) a quarter and half a million pounds. It stands, in *daily* rations of bread alone, for nearly 200 sacks of wheat; in material equipment—initial, apart from ammunition—it stands in weapons and machines for at least another quarter of a million, in *ready* ammunition of small arms for at least £80,000, in shell for as much again.

To all this conception of scale you must add two more points. The soldier is moved in a way that the civilian is not. He is given at the expense of the State and not for his pleasure, the equivalent of a great quantity of lengthy excursions. He is taken across the sea, brought back on leave or in convalescence, moved from place to place by train or by mechanical traction, and all that upon a scale quite out of proportion to the narrow limits of his travel during civilian occupation. Within six months hundreds of thousands of Englishmen have been conveyed to the heart of France, moved again in that country over a space of more than a hundred miles, and a considerable proportion of them brought back and sent out again in the interval. Lastly, there is the indeterminate but heavy medical expense.

The second and last point in this consideration of scale is the enormously expensive element of uncertainty. It would be expensive enough to have to arrange for so much movement and so much clothing and equipment upon a wholly novel and increased scale, if we knew exactly what that movement and that equipment was to be—if, so to speak, you could take the problem *statically* and work out its details in an office as you work out the costings of a great shop or factory. But it is in the essence of an army that it should be mobile, moving suddenly and as quickly as possible where it is wanted, with no power of prediction as to how those moves may develop. You are "in" therefore, for an unknown factor of expense over and above the novelty and very high cost of the economic energy you suddenly bring into play with war. And that unknown factor is the extent to which you will be wasting and moving.

If considerations such as these give us some idea of the *scale* of supply, a further series of considerations will help us to appreciate the *rate* or *pace* at which the stream of supply must flow.

There are several ways in which this can be graphically presented through examples. Here are a few.

Great Britain controls half of the shipping of the world. She engages in the present war and part of her floating mercantile resources is suddenly required for the campaign. Those ships have to be constantly steaming, consuming coal, provisions for their crews, materials for repairs, at a far higher rate than their civilian use demanded; and the thing translates itself to the ordinary citizen in the shape of vastly increased freights and consequently increased prices for the imports received by this island.

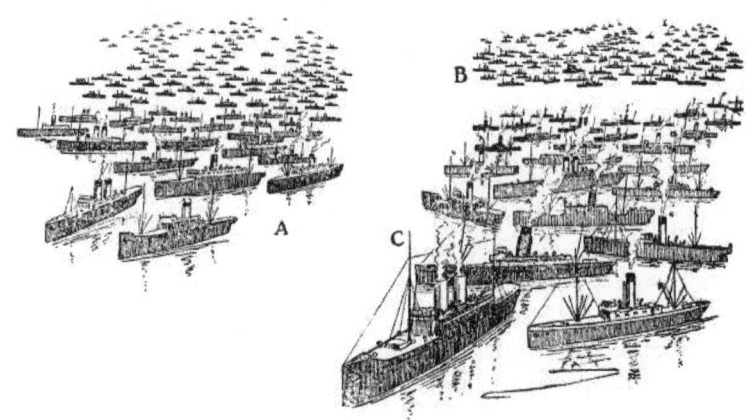

DIAGRAM III. Great Britain controls half the shipping of the world. She engages in war, and a part of her floating mercantile resources is suddenly required for the campaign. Those ships have to be constantly steaming, consuming coals, provisions, etc., at a far higher rate than their civilian use demanded; and the thing translates itself to the ordinary citizen in the shape of increased freights, and consequently increased prices for imports. The groups A, B and C combined represent the shipping of the world—A being foreign shipping. B and C together represent the whole of the British shipping, while the group C by itself represents the portion detached for the purposes of the war.

Here is another example. This country is as highly industrialized as any in the world. It is particularly fitted for the production of mechanical objects, and especially for mechanical objects in metal, yet suppose that even this country were asked suddenly (with no more than the plant it had before the war) to equip such a force as that with which the French defended their country last August—not to equip it with ammunition but with weapons and auxiliary machinery alone; the performance of such a task would have taken all the arms factories of Great Britain more than two years.

Take the rate of expenditure of ammunition. In considering this element in the pace or rate of supply we must remember the moments in which waste at the front becomes abnormal. A rapid retirement like the retreat from Mons means the loss of material wholesale. A favourable moment seized, as September 6 was seized, for the counter-offensive, which is known as "The Battle of the Marne," means such an expenditure of ammunition as was never provided for in any of the text-books or considered possible until this campaign was engaged.

Here is an example. The Germans had prepared war for two years—prepared it specially for the particular moment in which they forced it upon Europe. Their first operations in France up to September 6 followed almost exactly the plan they had carefully elaborated. Nevertheless, we now know that whole groups of the enemy ran through the enormous supplies which were pouring in to their front, and that one element in the disarray of the first German army in those critical days was the shortage of shell, particularly for the heavy pieces.

It is generally reported, and it is probably true, that the enemy exhausted before the end of his great effort in the West (which lasted less than one hundred days, and the intensity of which was relaxed after the middle of November) *seven times* the heavy ammunition he had allowed for the whole campaign.

Here is another example. The life of a horse in the South African War was, I believe, not quite as many *weeks* as the same animal had expectation of *years* in civilian occupation.

DIAGRAM IV. A troop train is a very long train, and it is packed close with men. To move one Army Corps alone (without the cavalry) you must allow over 180 such trains. The diagram gives you an idea of what that means.

Here is yet another example, connected with the transport. A troop train is a very long train, and it is packed close with men. For the transport of animals and of material objects every inch of space available is calculated and used. Well, to move one Army Corps alone (without the cavalry) you must allow over 180 such trains. Now, even at the origin of the war, upon one front alone, before the numbers had fully developed, the German invasion involved at least twenty-five Army Corps.

Such an appreciation of the scale and the pace of supply is sufficient to illuminate one's third point, the delicacy of the whole business, and the peril of its embarrassment. You are feeding, munitioning, clothing, evacuating the wounded from, sheltering, and equipping millions of men; those millions subject to sudden abnormal periods of wastage, any one of which may come at any unexpected moment, and further subject to sudden unforeseen movements upon any scale. You must so co-ordinate all your movements of supply that no part of the vast line is pinched even for twenty-four hours.

The whole process may be compared to the perpetual running of millions of double threads, which reach from every soldier back ultimately to the central depots of the army, and thence to the manufactories, and these double threads perpetually working back and forth from the manufactories to the Front. These double threads—always travelling back and forth, remember—are gathered into a vast number of small, local centres, the sheaves or cords so formed are gathered back again to some hundreds of greater centres, and these ropes again concentrated upon some dozens of main bases of supply. And the ends of these threads—though all in continual movement back and forth—must each be kept taut, must cross sometimes one over the other in a complicated pattern perpetually requiring readjustment, while all the time now one, now another group of threads suddenly sets up a heavy strain, where the men to whom they relate are engaged in particularly violent action.

To keep such a web untangled, duly stretched, and accurately working is an effort of organization such as will never be seen in civilian life, and such as was never seen, even in military life, until modern times.

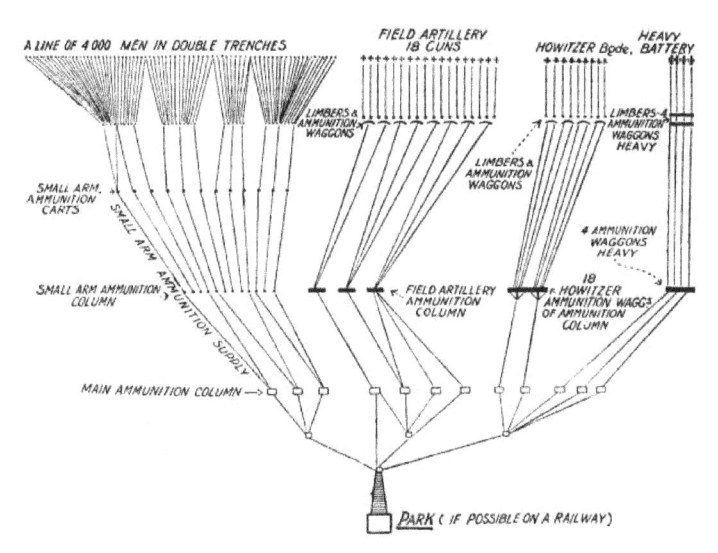

DIAGRAM V. An important point in connexion with supply is the delicacy of the whole business and the peril of its embarrassment. The diagram concerns only one tiny detail of the process—no more than the supply of ammunition to one part of a division out of the hundreds of divisions that build up an army. It shows how the ammunition is sorted and distributed from an ammunition park to the men in the front line; the complexity under actual conditions of service being apt to be far more tangled and diversified, according to circumstances.

Observe the fifth diagram, which concerns only one tiny detail of the process; no more than the supply of ammunition (out of all that has to be supplied) and no more than the ammunition of one part of a division (excluding cavalry) out of the hundreds of divisions and more that build up one of these great national armies. Even that diagram, complex as it is, does not nearly represent the whole complexity even of so small a fraction, but is sufficient to illustrate my case.

Such a machine or organization, by which an army lives, and in the collapse of which an army rapidly ceases to be, is clearly at the mercy of the least disorder. It is indeed protected by the most careful dispositions, and everything is done to safeguard its gathering strands, as they unite towards the base, from interruption. But conceive what the effect of such interruption would be, or even the menace of it! Deduce from this the importance where such a vast body of men is concerned, of *freedom from embarrassment* in the minds of those who have to direct the operation of the almost infinite skein!

It is this point, the peril of embarrassment, which is—at the moment in which I am writing these lines—of such capital importance in connection with the question of blockade. We may blockade an enemy's resources and say: "With very careful economy he has food for nine-tenths of the year"; or, "Though already anxious for the future, he has sufficient copper for his shell and cartridge cases for some time to come"; or, "Though already the Government is forbidding the sale of petrol, the enemy can, for some time to come, supply his mechanical transport." But the mere numerical calculation of his decreasing resources is no guide to the moral disorder which the peril alone may cause. The elasticity of the whole machine is at once affected from the mere knowledge that abnormal economy is demanded. The directing brain of it is disturbed in an increasing degree as civilian necessities mix with the already severe strain upon the supplies of the army.

To produce such a confusion, moral as well as material, is the directing motive of blockade, and the success of such a policy begins long before the point of grave material embarrassment is reached.

It is on this account that nations fighting with their whole strength, as modern nations in competition with the detestable Prussian model are compelled to fight, must ultimately, willy-nilly, turn to the policy of complete blockade, and that the success of this policy attempted by both parties to a struggle—necessarily better achieved by one than by the other—will perhaps more largely than anything else determine—seeing what the complexity of national commerce now is—the issue of a great modern war.

WAR TO-DAY AND YESTERDAY

This war, in many ways, is quite different from any war in the past. The length of defensive lines, the development of field fortification and of big guns, and other important matters are dealt with in the following pages.

WAR TO-DAY AND YESTERDAY

THERE has appeared in the present campaign a number of situations so different both from what was known of war in the past and from what was expected of any great modern war in West Europe that opinion upon the change is confused and bewildered. Sometimes it is thrown right out of its bearings by the novelties it witnesses. And, what is more grave, opinion is sometimes led to misjudge altogether the nature of war by these novelties.

For instance, you find people telling you that a war such as this can end in a "draw" or stalemate. They say this foolish thing simply because they are impressed by the present unexpected and apparently unprecedented phase of the war.

Or, again, people tell you vaguely that "the question of finance will end the war," because they are bewildered by the magnitude of the figures of expense, forgetting that the only five things a nation needs in order to prosecute war are men, arms, clothing, shelter and food, and, these things being provided, the whole hotch-potch of reality and imagination which is called finance is indifferent to it.

Now, to prevent false judgments of that kind and the misleading of public opinion, there is nothing more useful than to distinguish between the things in which modern war between great forces, fought with modern weapons and by men trained to utilize their powers to the utmost, differs from and resembles the wars of the past.

Let us begin with the differences.

When you are dealing with many miles of men whose armament is not only destructive at a great distance, but also over a wide belt of ground, you have, in the first place, a vast extension of any possible defensive lines. It is in this, perhaps, that the present war is most sharply distinguished from the wars of the past; and I mean by the wars of the past the wars of no more than a generation ago.

There have been plenty of long defensive lines in the past. Generals desiring to remain entirely upon the defensive, for any reason, over an indefinite space of time (for no one can remain on the defensive for ever), have constructed from time immemorial long lines behind which their men, though very thinly spread out, could hold against the enemy.

They have been particularly led to do this since the introduction of firearms, because firearms give the individual man a wider area over which he can stop his enemy. But in every form of war, primitive or modern, these great lines have existed.

The Wall of China is one great instance of them; the Roman Wall over the North of Britain, from sea to sea, is another; and the long-fortified Roman frontier from the Rhine to the Danube was a third.

The generals of Louis XIV, in a line called by the now famous name of La Bassée, established on a smaller scale the same sort of thing for a particular campaign. There are hundreds of examples. But the characteristic novelty of the present war, and the point in which it differs from all these ancient examples, is the *rapidity* with which such lines are established by the great numbers now facing each other, armed as they are by weapons of very long range.

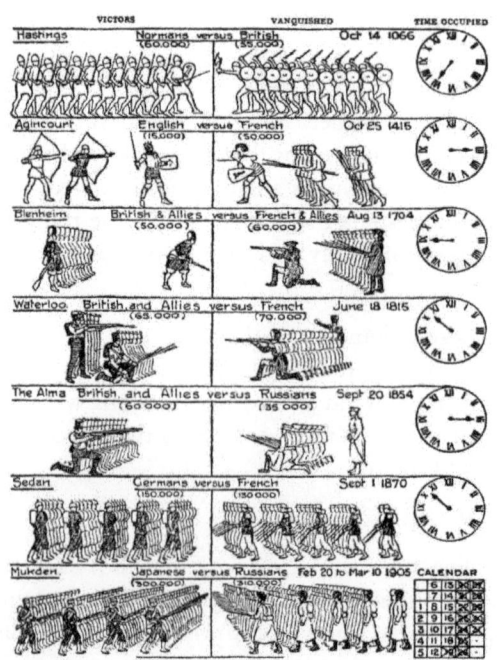

This gives you at a glance an idea of the numbers engaged and the time occupied in some famous battles of the past. Each little figure in the above drawings represents 5000 men. It will be seen that even the Battle of Mukden is scarcely comparable in duration with the months-long contests of the present war.

Forty-eight hours' preparation, or even less, is enough for troops to "dig themselves in" over a stretch of country which, in the maximum case of the French lines, is 300 miles in extent. Every slight advance is guaranteed by a new construction of trenches, every retirement hopes to check the enemy at another line of trenches established at the rear of the first.

Roughly speaking, half a million of men could hold one hundred miles of such a line under modern conditions, and, therefore, when the vast numbers which such a campaign as this produces are brought into the field, you can establish a line stretching across a whole continent and incapable of being turned.

That is what has been done in France during the present war. You have got trenches which, so long as they are sufficiently held in proportion to the numbers of the offensive, are impregnable, and which run from the Swiss Mountains to the North Sea.

It is possible that you may have to-morrow similar lines running from the Carpathians to the Baltic. Though this I doubt, first, because in the Eastern theatre of war Russia can produce perpetually increasing numbers to assault those lines; secondly, because the heavy artillery essential for their support cannot be present in large numbers in the East.

One may sum up, therefore, upon this particular novel feature of the present campaign and say that it is mainly due to the very large numbers engaged, coupled with the retaining power of the heavy artillery which the Germans have prepared in such high numerical superiority over their opponents. It is not a feature which you will necessarily find reproduced by any means in all the wars, even of the near future, or in the later stages of this war.

You must be able, as you retreat, to check your enemy appreciably before you can trace such a line; you must be able to hammer him badly with heavy guns stronger than his own while you are making it, and unless you are present in very great numbers you will only be able to draw it over a comparatively short line which your enemy may be able to turn by the left or the right.

Still, it may be of interest to compare the length of lines thus drawn apparently during the course of a campaign in the past with those drawn in the course of the present campaign, and in the first diagram I show the contrast. It is striking enough.

Another novel feature in which this war differs even from the Balkan War is the new value which has been given to howitzer fire, and in particular to its domination over permanent fortification. This is perhaps the most important of all the changes which this war has introduced into military art and it is worth while understanding it clearly. Its main principles are simple enough.

Mankind at war has always used devices whereby he has been able with a small number to detain the advance of a larger number. That, for instance, was the object of a castle in the Middle Ages. You built a stronghold of stone which the engines of that time could not batter down or undermine save at a very great expense of time, and you were certain that for every man able to shoot an arrow from behind such defences ten men or more would be needed for the work of trying to batter them down. So when you knew that your enemy would have to go through a narrow pass in the mountains, let us say, or across an important ford of a river, you built a castle which, as the military phrase goes, "commanded" that passage; that is, you devised a stronghold such that with, say, only 1000 of your men you would quite certainly hold up 10,000 of your enemy.

If your enemy passed by without taking your castle the thousand men inside could sally out and cut off his supplies as they passed down the mountain road or across the ford, and so imperil his main forces that had gone forward.

Your stronghold would never, of course, suffice to win a war—its function was purely negative. You could not attack with it; you could not destroy your enemy with it. But you could *gain time* with it. You could check your enemy in his advance while you were gathering further men to meet him, and sometimes you could even wear him out in the task of trying to reduce the stronghold.

Now the whole history of the art of war is a history of the alternate strength and weaknesses of these *permanent fortifications*; the word *permanent* means fortifications not of a temporary character, hurriedly set up in the field, but solidly constructed over a long space of time, and destined to permit a prolonged resistance.

```
━━━━ Lines of Torres Vedras. (Peninsular War.)
━━━━ Lines of Wissembourg 1793.
━━━━ Lines of La Bassée 1709-11.

━━━━━━━━━━━━━━━━━━━━━━━━━━━━━━━━━━━━━━━━━━━
     The Present lines in France from the Swiss Frontier to the North Sea. 1914.
```

DIAGRAM I. A striking comparison of the length of lines in some past campaigns with the present. The characteristic novelty of the present war is the rapidity with which such lines are established by the great numbers now facing each other, armed as they are by weapons of very long range.

When cannon came and gunpowder for exploding mines underground, the mediæval castle of stone could be quickly reduced. There was, therefore, a phase in which permanent fortification or permanent works were at a discount. The wars of Cromwell in this country, for instance, were fought in the middle of such a phase. The castles went down like nine-pins. But the ingenuity of man discovered a new form of defence valuable even against cannon, in the shape of scientifically constructed *earthworks*. The cannon ball of the day could not destroy these works, and though they could be *sapped* and *mined*, that is, though tunnels could be dug in beneath them and explosives there fired to their destruction, that was a long business, and the formation of the works was carefully designed to give the garrison a powerful advantage of fire over the besiegers.

Works of this kind made the defensive strong again for more than two hundred years. Just as there used to be a stone wall surrounding a town, at intervals from which people could shoot sideways along the "curtain" or sheer wall between the towers, so now there was earthwork, that is, banks of earth backed by brick walls to hold them up, and having a ditch between the outer parapet and the inner. These earthworks were star-shaped, sending out a number of projecting angles, so that an attack launched upon any point would receive converging fire from two points of the star, and the entrances were further protected by outer works called horn works.

With the war of 1870, and even for somewhat before it, it was found that the increased range of modern artillery had destroyed the value of these star-shaped earthworks, taking the place of the old walls round a town. One could batter the place to pieces with distant guns. Though the guns within the place were as strong as the guns outside, they were at this disadvantage: that they were confined within a comparatively small space which the besiegers could search by their fire, while the guns of the besiegers could not be equally well located by the gunners of the besieged within the fortress.

So the next step was to produce what has been known as the *Ring Fortress*. That is, a series of detached forts lying three or four miles outside the inner place of stores, barracks, etc., which you wanted to defend. Each fort supporting the two others next to it on either side of this ring was thought to be impregnable, for each fort was built within range of the two nearest, and on such a model were built Toul, Verdun, Epinal, Belfort, Metz, Strassburg, Thorn, Cracow, and fifty other great modern strongholds.

The theory that these ring fortresses could hold out indefinitely was based upon the idea that the fort so far out from the fortress would keep the enemy's guns too far away to damage the inner place of stores and garrison, and that the supporting fire of the various forts would prevent anyone getting between them. The three systems—first the stone wall, then the earthwork, then the ring fortress, are roughly expressed in the second diagram.

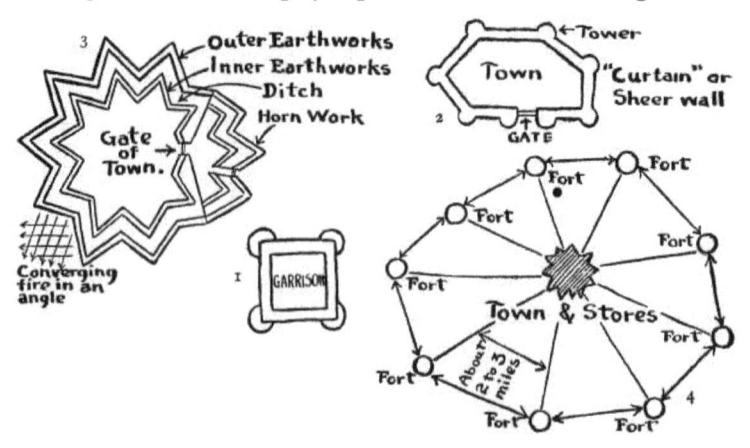

DIAGRAM II. Mankind at war has always used devices whereby he has been able with a small number to detain the advance of a larger number. Some of these systems are roughly expressed above. 1. The old stone fortress or castle of the Middle Ages. 2. The wall round a town. 3. The earthworks of a fortress of the period 1620-1860. 4. The "Ring" Fortress (1860-1914)—a series of detached forts lying three or four miles outside the inner place of stores, barracks, etc., which it was desired to defend.

Well, the chief lesson, perhaps, of the present war is that these ring fortresses fall quickly to howitzer fire. Each of the individual forts can be easily reduced by howitzer fire. This is concentrated against certain of the forts, which quickly fall, and once their ring is broken the result is equivalent to the breach in the wall of a fortress, and the whole stronghold falls. That is because in quite recent years two new factors have come in: (1) the mobile heavy howitzer; (2) the highest kinds of explosives.

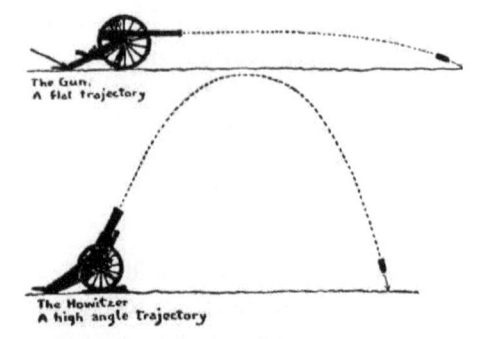

DIAGRAM III. A howitzer is a gun with a shorter barrel than the ordinary gun, and designed not to shoot its projectile more or less straight across the earth, as an ordinary gun does, but to lob it high up so that it falls almost perpendicularly upon its target.

A howitzer is a gun with a shorter barrel than the ordinary gun (and therefore lighter in proportion to the width of the shell, and so to the amount of the explosive it can fire) and designed not to shoot its projectile more or less straight across the earth, as an ordinary gun does, but to lob it high up so that it falls more or less perpendicularly upon its target.

Thus the German 11.2-inch howitzer, of which we have heard so much in this war, has a maximum range when it is elevated to 43 degrees, or very nearly half-way between pointing flat and pointing straight up—and howitzers can be fired, of course, at a much higher angle than that if necessary.

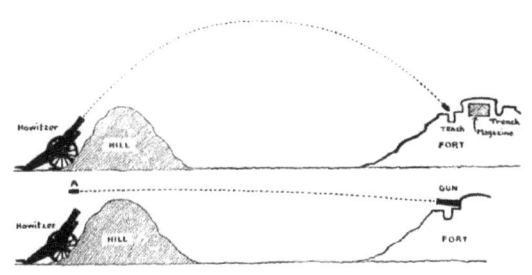

DIAGRAM IV. You can hide a howitzer behind a hill. The gun, though it has a longer range than the howitzer, can only get at the howitzer indirectly by firing over the point where it supposes the howitzer to be, as at A. Secondly, the howitzer can drop its shell into a comparatively narrow trench which the projectile of the gun will probably miss.

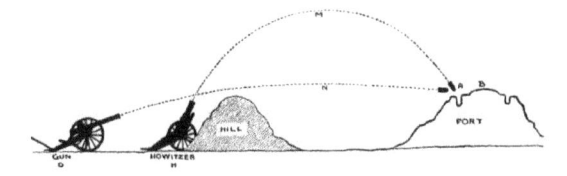

DIAGRAM V. If you want to make your shell fall into a trench of a fortification, A, or come down exactly on the top of the shelter in a fort, B, it is obvious that your howitzer, firing from H, and lobbing a projectile along the high-angle trajectory M, will have a much better chance of hitting it than your gun G, sending a projectile further indeed but along the flatter trajectory N.

The advantage of the howitzer is two-fold.

In the first place, you can hide it behind a hill or any other form of obstacle or screen, as it shoots right up in the air. A gun which fires more or less flat along the earth cannot get at it.

The gun, though it has a longer range than the howitzer, can only get at the howitzer indirectly by firing over the point where it supposes the howitzer to be, as at A in Diagram IV, and so timing the fuse that the shell bursts exactly there.

Now, that is a difficult operation, both because it is difficult to spot a machine which you cannot see, and though modern time fuses are very accurate, they cannot, of course, be accurate to a yard.

Secondly, the howitzer can drop its shell into a comparatively narrow trench, which the projectile of a gun with its flat trajectory will probably miss. If you want to make your shell fall into a trench of a fortification or come down exactly on the top of the shelter in a fort, as at A, the trench in the fifth diagram, or at B, the shelter, it is obvious that your howitzer firing from H, and lobbing a projectile along the high-angle trajectory M, will have a much better chance of hitting it than your gun G, sending a projectile further, indeed, but along the flatter trajectory N.

Of course, another howitzer within the fortifications could, in theory, lob a shell of its own over the hill and hit the besieging howitzer, but in practice it is very easy for the besieging howitzer to find out exactly where the vulnerable points of the fortress are—its trenches and its shelter and magazine—and very difficult for the people in the fortress to find out where the howitzer outside is. Its place is marked upon no map, and it can move about, whereas the fortress is fixed.

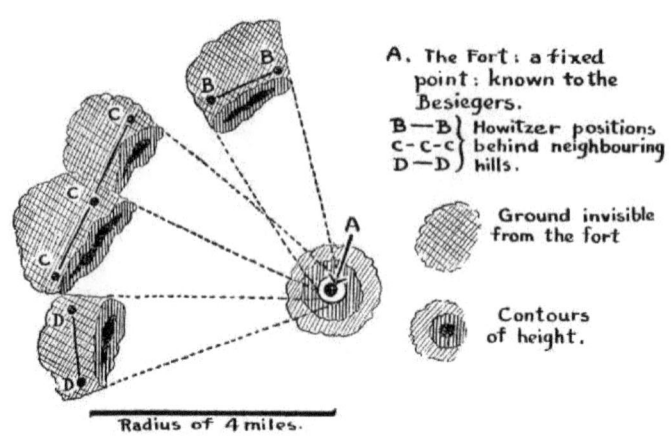

DIAGRAM VI. The fort on an elevation at A, and confined within a narrow space, is a target for howitzers placed anywhere behind hills at, say, four miles off—as at B-B, C-C, D-D. It is difficult enough for the fort to find out where the howitzer fires from in any case; furthermore, the howitzer can shift its position anywhere along the lines B-B, C-C, and D-D.

Look, for instance, at Diagram VI.

The fort on an elevation at A, and confined within a narrow space, is a target for howitzers placed anywhere behind hills at, say, four miles off, as at B-B, C-C, D-D. It is difficult enough for the fort to find out where the howitzer fires from in any case, and even when it has spotted this the howitzer can move anywhere along the lines B-B, C-C, or D-D, and shift its position.

Further, be it remembered that under quite modern conditions the accuracy of the howitzer fire against the fort can be checked by aeroplanes circulating above the fort, whereas the fort is a poor starting-place for corresponding aeroplanes to discover the howitzer.

But while the howitzer has this advantage, it has the grave disadvantage of not having anything like the same range as the gun, size for size. For a great many years it has been known that the howitzer has the advantage I have named. But, in spite of that, permanent fortification was built and could stand, for it was impossible to move howitzers of more than a certain small size. The explosives in those small shells did very great damage, but the fortress could, with its very heavy guns, keep the enemy out of range. But when large, and at the same time mobile howitzers were constructed which, though they fired shells of a quarter of a ton and more, could go along almost over any ground and be fired from almost anywhere, and moved at comparatively short notice from one place to another, it was another matter. The howitzer became dangerous to the fortress. When to this was added the new power of the high explosives, it became fatal to the fortress.

To-day the 11-inch howitzer, with a range of about six miles, capable of hiding behind any elevation and not to be discovered by any gun within the fortress, and, further, capable of being moved at a moment's notice if it is discovered, has the fortress at its mercy. Air reconnaissance directs the fire, and great masses of high explosives can be dropped, without serious danger to the besieger, upon the fortified permanent points, which are unable to elude great shells of high explosive once the range has been found.

Another development of the present war, and somewhat an unexpected one, has been the effect of the machine-gun, and this has depended as much upon the new German way of handling it behind a screen of infantry, which opened to give the machine-gun play, as to any other cause.

The fourth most obvious, and perhaps most striking change is, of course, the use of aircraft, and here one or two points should be noticed which are not always sufficiently emphasized. In the first place, the use of aircraft for scouting has given, upon the whole, more than was expected of it. It prevents the great concentration of troops unknown to the enemy at particular points on a line save in one important exception, which is the movement of troops by night over railways, and, indeed, this large strategical use of railways, especially in night movements, in the present war, is not the least of the novelties which it has discovered. But, on the other hand, aircraft has reintroduced the importance of weather in a campaign, and to some extent the importance of the season. When you doubtfully discovered your enemy's movements by "feeling" him with cavalry or gathering information from spies and prisoners, it made little difference whether the wind was high or low or whether you were in summer or in winter. But the airman can only work usefully by day, and in bad weather or very strong gales he cannot fly, which means that unexpected attack is to be dreaded more than ever by night, and that for the first time in many centuries the wind has again come to make a difference, as it did against the missile of the bow and arrow.

There are a great many other novel developments which this war has discovered, but these are, I think, the chief. It is advisable not only to discover such novelties, but also the permanent features, which even modern machinery and modern numbers have not changed. Of these you have first the elementary feature of *moral*.

Ultimately, all Europeans have much the same potential *moral*. Different types of drill and different experiences in war, a different choice of leaders and the rest of it produce, however, different *kinds of moral*; different excellencies and weaknesses. Now in this department much the most remarkable general discovery in the war has been the endurance and steadiness under loss of conscript soldiers.

It had always been said during the long peace that modern conscript short-service soldiers would never stand the losses their fathers had stood in the days of professional armies, or longer service, or prolonged campaigns such as those of the Napoleonic wars. But to this theory the Manchurian campaign gave a sufficient answer if men would only have heeded it; the Balkan War a still stronger one, while the present war leaves no doubt upon the matter.

The short-service conscript army has in this matter done better than anything that was known in the past. Of particular reasons perhaps the most interesting and unexpected has been the double surprise in the German use of close formation. It was always taken for granted, both by the German school and by their opponents, that close formation, if it could be used in the field at all, would, by its rapidity and weight, carry everything before it.

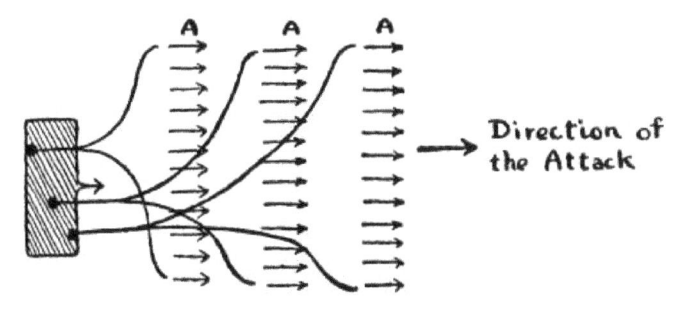

DIAGRAM VII. You have here 1000 men ready to attack. If they attack in long open waves of men as at A-A, it takes them a long time to spread out, and when they are spread out the effect of their shock is not overwhelming.

You have in Diagram VII a thousand men ready to attack. If they attack in long open waves of men as at A-A, it takes them a long time to spread out, and when they are spread out the effect of their shock is not overwhelming. They can only succeed by wave following wave.

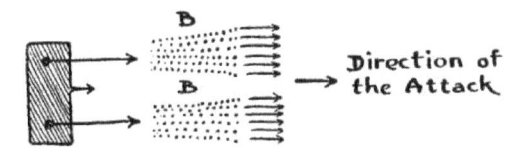

DIAGRAM VIII. If your 1000 men attack in denser bodies as at B-B, they can be launched much more quickly, and the effect of their shock when they come on is much greater.

If they attack in denser bodies (Diagram VIII), as at B-B, they can be launched much more quickly, and the effect of their shock when they come on is much greater; it is, to use the German's own term, the effect of a swarm.

This seemed obvious, but the critics of the second system of close or swarm formation always said that, though they admitted its enormous power if it could be used at all, it could not be used because its losses would be so enormous against modern firearms. Your spread-out line, as at A-A, offered but a small target, and the number of men hit during an assault would be far less than the number hit in the assault of such bodies as B-B, which presented a full target of dense masses.

Well, in the event, that criticism proved wrong in *both* its conceptions. The Germans, thanks to their great courage and excellent discipline, *have* been able to use close formations. The immense losses these occasion have not prevented their continuous presence in the field, but, contrary to all expectations, they have not, as a rule, got home. In other words, they have, in the main, failed in the very object for which the heavy sacrifice they entail was permitted.

Another unexpected thing in which this war has warranted the old conception of arms is the exactitude of provision. Everybody thought that there would be a great novelty in this respect, and that the provisioning of so many men might break down, or, at any rate, hamper their mobility. So far from this being the case, the new great armies of this modern war have been better and more regularly provisioned than were the armies of the past, and this is particularly true upon the side of the Allies, even in the case of that astonishing march of three million of Russians across Poland with the roads in front of them destroyed and the railway useless.

WHAT TO BELIEVE IN WAR NEWS

Showing how the reports in the Press should be selected and compared, so as to arrive at a just estimate of the true position of affairs.

WHAT TO BELIEVE IN WAR NEWS

THE other day there came a message to London from Italy, solemnly delivered in printer's ink and repeated in nearly every newspaper, that the town of Cracow was invested, that the bombardment had begun, and that part of the city was in flames.

Cracow is the key of Silesia, and Silesia is the Lancashire of Prussia. The successful investment of Cracow would certainly bring the war to its last phase, and that phase one bringing rapid victory to the Allies.

But Cracow was not invested; no one had bombarded it. The whole thing was fantastic nonsense.

So much for one particular newspaper report, which had nothing to distinguish it from other telegrams and news, and which millions of people must have read and believed.

Every one of the readers of these lines will be able to recall other instances of the same kind. I have before me as I write extract after extract of that sort. In one, Roulers has been retaken; in another, Lille is reoccupied; in another (a much earlier one), the Germans are at Pont Oise.

Sometimes these accounts appear in long and detailed descriptions proceeding from the pens of men who are fairly well known in Fleet Street, and who have the courage to sign their names.

There has, perhaps, never been a great public occasion in regard to which it was more necessary that men should form a sound judgment, and yet there has certainly not been one in our time upon which the materials for such a judgment have been more confused.

The importance of a sound public judgment upon the progress of the war is not always clearly appreciated. It depends upon truths which many men have forgotten, and upon certain political forces which, in the ordinary rush and tumble of professional politics, are quite forgotten. Let me recall those truths and those forces.

The truths are these: that no Government can effectively exercise its power save upon the basis of public opinion. A Government can exercise its power over a conquered province in spite of public opinion, but it cannot work, save for a short time and at an enormous cost in friction, counter to the opinion of those with whom it is concerned as citizens and supporters. By which I do not mean that party politicians cannot act thus in peace, and upon unimportant matters. I mean that no kind of Government has ever been able to act thus in a crisis.

It is also wise to keep the mass of people in ignorance of disasters that may be immediately repaired, or of follies or even vices in government which may be redressed before they become dangerous.

It is always absolutely wise to prevent the enemy in time of war from learning things which would be an aid to him. That is the reason why a strict censorship in time of war is not only useful, but essentially and drastically necessary. But though public opinion, even in time of peace, is only in part informed, and though in time of war it may be very insufficiently informed, yet upon it and with it you govern. Without it or against it in time of war you cannot govern.

Now if during the course of a great war men come quite to misjudge its very nature, the task of the Government would be strained some time or other in the future to breaking point. False news, too readily credited, does not leave people merely insufficiently informed, conscious of their ignorance, and merely grumbling because they cannot learn more, it has the positive effect of putting them into the wrong frame of mind, of making them support what they should not support, and neglect what they should not neglect.

Unfortunately, public authority, which possesses and rightfully exercises so much power in the way of censorship—that is, in the way of limiting information—has little power to correct false information. The Censor receives a message, saying that at the expense of heavy loss General So-and-So's brigade, composed of the Downshires and the Blankshires, repelled the enemy upon such-and-such a front, but that three hundred men are missing from the brigade at the end of the action. If he allows this piece of news to go through at all he must even so refuse to allow any mention of the names of the regiments, of their strength, of the place where they were fighting, and the numbers of those who are missing.

Why must the Censor act thus? Because this information would be of the utmost value to the enemy. The enemy, remember, does not ever quite know what is in front of him. Indeed, the whole of military history consists in the story of men who are successful because they can gauge better than other men the forces which they have to meet.

Now if you let him know that on such-and-such an occasion the force that he met upon such-and-such a front was a brigade of infantry, and if you let him know its composition, and if you do this kind of thing with regard to the army in general, you end by letting him know two things which he particularly wants to know, and which it is all your duty to prevent him knowing. You let him know the size of the force in front of him, and you let him know its composition.

Similar reasons make the Censor hide from the enemy the number of men missing. The enemy knows if he has taken in prisoners wounded and unwounded two hundred and fifty men, and, for all he knows, that is, excepting the dead, your total loss; but if you publish the fact that you have lost a thousand men, he is accurately informed of a weakness in your present disposition, which he otherwise would not suspect.

All this action of the Censor is as wise as it is necessary, but in the face of false news he is in another position. In the first place, it is difficult for him to judge it (unless, of course, it concerns our own particular forces). In the second place, it may not concern matters which the enemy can possibly ignore. For instance, in this example of the supposed investment of Cracow. The Russians were certainly approaching the place. The news might conceivably be true. If it were true, the enemy would already be amply acquainted with it, and it would be of a nature not to aid him, but to discourage him. But the news was, in fact, untrue, and, being untrue, its publication did not a little harm.

Now, how are we to counter this danger? How is the plain man to distinguish in his news of the war what is true from what is false, and so arrive at a sound opinion? After some months of study in connexion with my work upon the three campaigns, I may be able to suggest certain ways in which such a position should be approached.

In the first place, the bases of all sound opinion are the official communiqués read with the aid of a map.

When I say "the official communiqués" I do not mean those of the British Government alone, nor even of the Allies alone, but of *all* the belligerents. You must read impartially the communiqués of the Austro-Hungarian and of the German Governments together with those of the British Government and its Allies, or you will certainly miss the truth. By which statement I do not mean that each Government is equally accurate, still less equally full in its relation; but that, unless you compare all the statements of this sort, you will have most imperfect evidence; just as you would have very imperfect evidence in a court of law if you only listened to the prosecution and refused to listen to the defence. Now, these official communiqués have certain things in common by whatever Government they are issued. There are certain features in them which you will always find although they come from natures as different as those of a Prussian staff officer and a Serbian patriot.

These common features we may tabulate thus:

> (*a*) Places named as occupied by the forces of the Government in question are really occupied. To invent the occupation of a town or point not in one's own hands would serve no purpose. It would not deceive the enemy and it would not long support opinion at home. Thus, when Lodz was reported occupied by the Germans in the middle of December, all careful students of the war knew perfectly well that the news was true.
>
> (*b*) Numbers, when they are quoted in connexion with a really ascertainable fact, and with regard to a precise and concrete circumstance, are nearly always reliable; though their significance differs, as I shall show in a moment, very greatly according to the way they are treated. Thus, if a Government says, "in such-and-such a place or on such-and-such a day we took three thousand prisoners," it is presumably telling the truth, for the enemy who has lost those prisoners knows it as well as they do. But estimates of what has happened in the way of numbers, where the Government issuing the estimate can have no direct knowledge, are quite another matter. These are only gathered from prisoners or from spies, and are often ridiculously wrong.
>
> (*c*) All official communiqués of whatever Government conceal reverses, save in minor points. They are wise to do this because there is no need to tell the enemy more than he may know of his own success. Reverses are not actually denied. They are omitted. Witness all omission of Lemberg from Austrian or German communiqués and, until somewhat late, of Tannenberg in Russian, of Metz in French official accounts.

Those are the three points which all the official communiqués have in common, and by bearing them well in mind we can often frame an accurate picture, in spite of the apparent contradiction and confusion which the reading of several communiqués one after the other produces.

For instance, the Germans are trying to cross the Bzura River according to the Russian communiqué of Saturday. Next Wednesday the Russian communiqué says, "Two attempts to cross the Bzura at such-and-such places were repelled"; while the German communication says, "Our troops succeeded in crossing the Bzura River at such-and-such a village and established themselves upon the right bank." In such a case the reader will be wise to believe the German communiqué and to take it for granted that while the Russians have repelled certain other attempts of the enemy to cross, this attempt has succeeded. But if the Germans go on to say, "The Russians retired after suffering losses which cannot have been less than twenty thousand," that is no news at all. It is obviously conjecture.

The various Governments issuing the communiqués have acquired certain habits in them which are worth noting if one is attempting to get at an accurate view of the war, and these habits may be briefly described as follows:

The British Government publishes short notes of advances made or of positions maintained, but very rarely refers to the losing of ground. It publishes casualty lists, which are, of course, not complete till very long after the events wherein the casualties were incurred. It supplements the short communiqués, and this by a more or less expanded narrative written by an official deputed for that purpose and giving accounts, often graphic, but necessarily of no military value; of no value, that is, for following the campaign. For if these narratives were of that kind the object of the censorship would be defeated.

The Belgian Government at the beginning of the war allowed very full accounts to go through and permitted the presence of correspondents at the front itself. That phase is now over and does not immediately concern us.

The French Government is by far the most reticent. It occasionally mentions the capture of a colour, but it publishes no casualty lists, no account of the field guns taken by French troops, and only now and then hints at the number of prisoners. It is, however, minutely accurate and even detailed in helping us to locate the fluctuations of the front, and by the aid of the French communiqués we can follow the war upon the map better than by the aid of any other. In its control of the Press the French General Staff is absolute. There has been nothing like it before, and it has been perfectly successful. You will see whole columns cut out of the newspapers in France and left blank, so certain are the military authorities of that country that the most vigorous censorship is vital to modern war. There is lastly to be noted in connexion with the French communiqués, especially after the first two months of the campaign, a remarkable frankness with regard to the occasional giving of ground by their own troops. The theory is that the enemy will know this in any case, and that as the position is secure, details of the sort though adverse, lend strength to the general narrative. In all this it must be remembered, of course, that the French Government, and, at this moment, the French Army, is far more powerful than any newspaper proprietor or other capitalist, and it is well for any nation at war to be able to say that.

The Russian Government is accurate, and, if anything, a little too terse in what it communicates to the public, but its censorship is far less strict than that of the French or even the English. Thus during the fighting round Lodz in defence of Warsaw at the beginning of December, correspondents from Petrograd were allowed to telegraph the most flamboyant descriptions of an immediately approaching German retreat which never took place. But, I repeat, the official Russian news is sober and restrained and accurate to a fault.

When we turn to the enemy's communiqués, we note first that the Austro-Hungarians are rare, insufficient, and confused. They are of little service, and may almost be neglected. But the German ones are numerous, extended and precise, and it is our particular business to judge them accurately if we are to understand the war, for when or if they tell the truth it is from them that we learn what would otherwise be hidden.

Well, in my judgment, these official German communiqués are in the main remarkably exact, and I believe it is possible to say why they are so exact. The German General Staff makes war in a purely mechanical fashion. It gravely exaggerates, as do all modern North Germans, the calculable element in human affairs. It is what used to be called "scientific." It is obvious that if you get a reputation for exactitude your falsehood, where it pays you to tell the falsehood, will be the more likely to work. The remarkable general accuracy of the official German communiqués cannot be due to any other object. It cannot be due to a mere love of truth, for the same Government deliberately circulates to its own provincial Press and to certain neutrals stories which cannot in the nature of things be true. Nor is this inaccuracy the result either of haste or of stupidity, it is very intelligent and obviously deliberate.

When, therefore, a German communiqué tells an untruth, that untruth is deliberate and upon an effective scale, and we have to consider what object it has, if we are to understand the news. We may take it that the object is nearly always domestic and political. Remember that these official German falsehoods, countersigned by the General Staff and the Government, are as rare as they are solid. They do not slip in. They are not vague or led up to by doubtful phrases.

Let me take two of them. Scarborough was officially described as a fortified port, like Sheerness or Cherbourg. That takes one's breath away. But monstrous as it is, it is not childish, because it was intended to give to the public that read it at home a certain effect which was, in fact, produced.

So successfully was that effect produced that a competent military critic in the German Press, writing the day after, had already got the idea that Scarborough was the most important naval base upon the East Coast. We must remember when we read such things that very few educated men out of a thousand in our own country could give the names of the fortified naval bases upon, say, the Adriatic, or even the Atlantic coast of France.

Another example of the same thing in a rather different line is the illumination of Berlin, the giving of a holiday to the school children and the official proclamation of a great and decisive victory in Poland during the course of the second battle for Warsaw, an action which had already lasted a fortnight, which was destined to last for many more days, and which remained at that time utterly undecided.

According to fairly reliable accounts of what was passing in Berlin at the moment, the Government was under some necessity of acting thus because the beginning of popular unrest had appeared. But whatever the cause, my point is that these German inaccuracies when they occur, which is rarely, are easily distinguishable. They stand out from the rest of the sober narrative by their conspicuous nonsense. They do not disturb the judgment of a careful reader. They should not prevent our continuing to collate most closely German statements in detail with those of the Allies, if we wish to understand the war.

There is one other point which I have already alluded to briefly, in which German communiqués may mislead, and that is in the way they handle statistics. The actual wording of news is often chosen in order to deceive, although the figures may be accurate. For instance, under the title "prisoners," the Germans include all wounded men picked up, all civilians which in this singular war are carried away into captivity, and, probably, when it is to their interest to swell the number of captured, they include certain numbers of the dead. In the same way they will talk of the capture of Verdun, and not infrequently include such of their own pieces as a re-advance has rediscovered upon the field.

It may be added in conclusion that while German communiqués rarely wander into conjecture, when they do they are idiotic, and exactly the same reason made German diplomats wholly misunderstand the mind of Europe immediately before the war. A German induction upon something other than material elements is worthless, and you see it nowhere more than in the careful but often useless, though monumental, work of German historians, who will accumulate a mass of facts greater in number than those of the scholars of any other nation, and then will draw a conclusion quite shamefully absurd; conclusions which, during the last forty years, have usually been followed by the dons of our own universities.

There is one last element for the formation of a sound opinion on the war which must be mentioned at the end of this, and that is the private evidence which occasionally but rarely comes through. Here there is no guide but that of one's own experience in travel, or that of one's own knowledge of the newspaper or the authority printing it. The occasions upon which such evidence is available are very infrequent, but when they do come the evidence is far more valuable than any official communiqué Let me quote as an example the letters from Hungary which appeared in the *Morning Post* upon various occasions during the autumn and early winter. They were quite invaluable.

Lastly, one might add for those who have the leisure and the confidence, the use of the foreign Press—especially the French and the German. It is biased, as is our own, and often belated in news. The German Press in particular suffers from the calculated policy of the Government of the German Empire, which at this moment believes it to be of service to stimulate public confidence of victory in every possible manner. Nevertheless, unless you do follow fairly regularly the Press of *all* the belligerent nations, you will obtain but an imperfect view of the war as a whole.

WHAT THE WAR HAS TAUGHT US

Many theories formulated in times of peace have crumbled in the face of recent actualities. Herein are set forth the main lessons to be learnt from the present war.

WHAT THE WAR HAS TAUGHT US

THE POINTS AT ISSUE

LONG periods of peace, intervening between cycles of war, are necessarily periods during which there must arise a mass of theory concerning the way in which men will be affected by war when it breaks out. They are necessarily periods in which are perfected weapons, the actual effect of which upon the human mind has not been tested. They are necessarily periods in which are perfected methods of defence, the efficiency of which against the corresponding weapons of offence remains a matter of doubt.

More than this, the whole business of naval and military strategy, though its fundamental rules remain unaltered, is affected by the use of new materials upon the full character of which men cannot finally decide until they come to action.

For instance, it is but a short while ago that a very eminent naval authority in this country put forward a defence of the submarine. This novel weapon had not been effectively used in war, though it has existed for so many years. He suggested that in the next naval war the battleship and cruiser would be rendered useless by the submarine, which would dominate all naval fighting.

His theory, which, of course, was only a theory, was very warmly contested. But between the two "schools" at issue nothing could decide but actual warfare at sea in which the submarine was used.

This necessary presence of rival "schools of thought" upon naval and military matters is particularly emphasized when the progress of invention is rapid, combined with the gradual perfecting of mechanical methods, and when the peace has been a long one.

Both these conditions have been present in Europe as a whole, and particularly in Western Europe, during our generation, and that is why this war has already taught so many lessons to those who study military and naval affairs, and why already it has settled so many disputed points.

Manœuvres could tell one much, but there was always absent from them the prime factor of fear, and that next factor almost as important, of actual destruction.

The list of questions, detailed and general, which have already been wholly or partly answered by the present campaigns might be indefinitely extended. There are hundreds of them. But if we consider only the principal ones we shall find that they fall roughly into two main categories. You have the technical questions of armament, its use and its effect; formation, and so forth; and you have the political questions.

The first set are concerned with the action of human beings under particular forms of danger, and the physical effect of the weapons they will employ under the conditions of a high civilization.

The second set are concerned with the action of human beings as citizens, not as soldiers. How they will face the advent of war, whether national feeling will be stronger than class feeling, whether secrecy can be preserved, and the rest.

A list of the principal points in each of these sets will run somewhat as follows:

In the first there were opposing schools as to—

(1) The value of modern permanent fortification and its power of resistance to a modern siege train.

(2) The best formation in which to organize troops for action, and particularly the quarrel between close formation and open.

(3) The doubts as to the degree of reliance which could be placed upon air-scouts, their capacity for engaging one another, the qualities that would give dominion of the air, and in particular the value of the great modern dirigible balloons.

(4) The effect, method, and proportionate value of rifle fire and of the bayonet.

(5) The use of field artillery; and particularly whether, after a certain degree of rapidity, still greater rapidity of fire was worth having.

(6) The exact *rôle* that would be played in modern war by the supply of certain materials hitherto unimportant and discoverable only in certain limited regions, most of them out of Europe. There are a great number of these materials, but much the most important is petrol.

(7) Lastly, and by far the most vital of purely technical questions to this country, was the solution of certain opposing theories upon what is rather

rhetorically called "the command of the sea" and what might more justly be called naval superiority.

In the second set, the political questions, the most important were:

(1) The working of the conscript and of the voluntary systems.

(2) The possibility of preserving secrecy.

(3) Whether mobilization would work smoothly or not in the face of class struggles supposedly formidable to national interests.

(4) The action of our modern town populations under the moral strain of war.

LESSONS WE HAVE LEARNT

Not all of the questions, military or political, have as yet been solved by experience. Many of them are, however, already partially solved, some wholly solved. And we may consider them usefully one by one.

(1) The value of permanent fortification.

Perhaps the most striking lesson of the war, and the one which is already conclusively taught by its progress, is the fact that modern permanent works, as we have hitherto known them at least, are dominated by modern siege artillery, and in particular by the mobile large howitzer using the last form of high explosive. It is here important to give the plain facts upon a matter which has from its suddenness and dramatic character given birth to a good many lessons.

Modern fortification has gone down after a very short resistance to howitzer fire, throughout the western field of the campaign. In general, if you can get the big, modern, mobile howitzer up to striking distance of modern permanent work, it batters that work to pieces within a period which will hardly extend over a week, and may be as short as forty-eight hours.

It is not a question of tenacity or courage. The greatest tenacity and the greatest courage can do nothing with a work that has been reduced to ruins, and in which there is no emplacement for a gun. So much is quite certain. But we must not run away with the idea either that this is the end of fortification for the future; temporary mobile batteries established *outside* the old permanent works will shield a garrison for an indefinite time. Nor is it true that the Germans have in this field any particular advantage save over the Russians, who are weak in their heavy artillery and have limited powers of increasing it. It will be discovered as the war proceeds that the Western armies are here in the same boat with the Germans.

It is true that the Germans have a larger howitzer than the French and the English. They have a few 420 millimetre howitzers, that is, guns of a calibre between 16 and 17 inches. But this gun is almost too large to use. What has done the work everywhere is the 11-inch howitzer, and a gun of much the same size is in possession of the French. Only hitherto the siege work has fallen to the German invaders. When and if the *rôles* are reversed, German permanent work will be just as vulnerable to French howitzer fire. And as for the abolition of fortification in future we need not look for that.

It is probable that the system of large, permanent enclosed works will give way to a system of narrow, prepared, parallel trenches connected by covered ways, which, by offering too small a target for accurate fire from a distance, and by being doubled and redoubled one behind the other, will be able to hold out far longer than the larger works which bore the brunt of the present war. But that the defensive will devise some means of meeting the new and unexpected powers of the offensive we may be certain, upon the analogy of all past warfare.

(2) In the matter of formation the surprise of the war has undoubtedly been the success of another German theory, to wit, the possibility of leading modern short-trained troops, against enormous losses, in close formation. Everywhere outside Germany that was doubted, and the Germans have proved that their initial contention was right, at least in their own case. But there is another aspect of this question which has as yet by no means been proved one way or the other, and that is, whether the very heavy losses this use of close formation entails are worth while in a campaign not immediately successful at the outset. We are not yet able to say how far troops once submitted to such violence can be brought to suffer it again—or how long after—nor are we able to say what effect this lavish expenditure of men has towards the end of a campaign if its primary object, immediate initial success, fails.

(3) In the matter of aircraft, four things have come out already.

(*a*) Men will engage each other in the air without fear and they will do so continually, appalling as the prospect seemed in its novelty before the outbreak of this war.

(*b*) Aircraft can discover the movement of troops in large bodies more accurately and successfully than had been imagined.

(*c*) That body of aircraft which is used to a rougher climate, and to working in heavier winds, will have an immense advantage not only in bad weather but in all weather. It is this, coupled with a very fine and already established tradition of adventure, which has made the English airmen easily the superior of their Allies and enemies.

(*d*) The aeroplane is neither as invulnerable at a great height as one school imagined it, nor as vulnerable as the opposite school maintained. The casualties are not as high in proportion to the numbers engaged as they would be in any other arm—at least so far—but they exist. And it would seem that the impossibility of telling whether an aeroplane belongs to friend or foe is a serious addition to the risk.

Many questions connected with aircraft still remain to be solved; by far the most important of which to this country are connected with the efficiency of the dirigible balloon.

(4) The amount of attention that should be given to good rifle firing and the importance that should be attached to the bayonet seem both to have been answered hitherto by the war.

Superior rifle fire, especially under the conditions of a difficult defensive, was the saving of the British force during the retreat from Mons, and, during the whole battle of the Marne, French accounts agree that the bayonet was the deciding factor in action after action. But even if it be true, in the words of a French officer, that "all actions end with the bayonet," the actual number of troops thus engaged and the casualties connected with them, are not in a very high proportion to the whole.

It almost seems as though the bayonet had replaced the old shock action of cavalry in some degree, and that it was to be used only when the opposing troops were shaken or were occupied in too precipitate a retirement. Of successful bayonet work against other conditions we have at least had no examples recorded.

(5) On the two chief points in connexion with field artillery, records hitherto received tell us little. We shall not know until more detailed accounts are available whether the vastly superior rapidity of fire enjoyed by the French 75 millimetre gun has given it a corresponding superiority over its opponent, the German 77. That it has a superiority is fairly clear. The degree of that superiority we shall not learn until we have the story of the war from the German side.

Neither are we established upon the question of weight. General Langlois' theory, which convinced the French that the light gun was essential, has not so far been proved absolutely certain, and there have been occasions when the English heavier gun (notably at Meaux) was of vast importance to our Allies. But I suggest that this question will be better answered now the weather has changed. In dry weather, that is, over hard ground, the difference between the heavier and the lighter gun is not so noticeable; once the ground is heavy it becomes very noticeable indeed.

(6) With the next question, that of the materials and their supply, we enter a region of the utmost interest to this country in particular, because it is the superiority of this country at sea, and the almost complete blockade of the Germanic Powers, that is here concerned. Roughly speaking, we find (*a*) That a blockade of enemy ports from a great distance is easy; (*b*) of enemy supply *through neutrals* very difficult indeed; (*c*) That certain special products which modern science has made necessary in war are most affected. For example:

Of the many things a modern army requires which are to be found only in a few special places, and those, most of them, out of Europe, the most important of all is petrol. It is obviously of capital importance for air work, and where you have a number of good roads, as in the Western field of operations, it is almost as important for transport work.

Now it so happens that petrol is not found in Western Europe at all. The European supply as a whole is limited, and is in the main confined to Galicia, Roumania, and Russia. The Asiatic and American supply is only available to Austria-Hungary and Germany by way of the ocean, and the ocean is closed to them. Russian supply, of course, they cannot obtain. Galician supply swings back and forth now in the possession of the Austrian and now in that of the Russian Army.

There remains only Roumania, and though Roumania is neutral it is doubtful or rather nearly certain that no sufficient supplies are coming into the Germanic Powers from that source. This is up to the moment of writing the chief effect of the British naval superiority, to which I will next turn.

(7) Most of the things that were said in time of peace about the effect of naval superiority or "command of the sea" have proved true. The blockade of the inferior naval powers is nearly complete—though it must be remembered that they have an exceedingly limited coastline, and that the problem will be very different against a large fleet possessed of many ports upon an extended coastline.

Further, the submarine has not proved itself as formidable against men-of-war as some thought, and the superiority of large craft is still admitted. On the other hand, it has been shown that a few hostile cruisers could continue to hold the seas for a much longer period than was imagined, and permanently to threaten commerce.

The conception that almost immediately after a declaration of war naval superiority would prevent the inferior naval power from commerce destroying, and that the trade routes of the superior power would be as safe as in time of peace has broken down. So has the idea that submarines could seek out the enemy's fleet in its ports and destroy them there.

The Political Results

When we turn to the political questions which the war has solved we have obtained immediate results of the very highest interest and importance, particularly to England.

In the first place, we have found that while the conscript system of war worked and mobilized with astonishing success, our own much more doubtful dependence upon a voluntary system for prolonged warfare has not betrayed this country. Everyone is agreed that the response to the call for volunteers, upon which there was at first great and legitimate anxiety, has been quite out of proportion to our expectations, and particularly to those of our enemies.

I think it true to say that there is nothing in which the German estimate of British psychology has been more hopelessly at sea than in this; and that the effects of this exceedingly rapid and large voluntary enlistment, principally drawn from the best material in the country, is the chief uncalculated factor in the scheme of what Germany expected to face. It is a factor that matures more slowly than many of the others, more slowly, perhaps, even than the effect of the blockade (which is also due to British effort), but it will mature with sufficient rapidity to affect all the later, and what may easily be the decisive, phases of the great war.

We have an equally direct answer to that hitherto quite uncertain question, whether in a modern state the secrecy which is essential to the success of a military plan could be maintained or no. Here again there has been a complete surprise. No one could have suggested six months ago that so news-tight a system could possibly have been worked with populations living in the modern great towns. And here it must be admitted that our opponents have done even better than ourselves. There is almost a comic element in the complete security with which the German and Austrian Governments can give those whom they govern exactly what news they choose and forbid the least scrap correcting or amplifying these meagre official statements, to pass the frontiers.

In connexion with this we should note that there is at the time of writing no definite answer to that very important question of how a complex modern town population will stand a heavy moral strain. But in so far as the indirect strain already caused by the war is any gauge, the answer seems to be favourable to the modern town liver.

Perhaps the most important point of all among the political questions which the war has propounded is that connected with class as against national feeling.

In plain fact, the idea that class feeling would anywhere in Europe be stronger than national feeling has proved utterly wanting.

In the industrial parts of Germany where the distinction of capitalist and proletariat was so clearly marked, that distinction had no effect whatsoever, not only upon mobilization, but upon the spirit of the troops; *a fortiori* it had none in that French society which is leavened by its peasantry, or in Russia which is almost wholly a peasant state.

There is nothing on which the judgment of an educated man would have proved more at sea had it been taken before the war broke out, and nothing in which the war has more poignantly revealed the ancient foundations upon which Europe reposes.

Milton Keynes UK
Ingram Content Group UK Ltd.
UKHW030850011224
451361UK00001B/118